Puzzle Pieces of My Heart

OUR STORIES OF ADOPTION

By Rosanne LeBaige

Puzzle Pieces of My Heart: Our Stories of Adoption

Trilogy Christian Publishers A Wholly Owned Subsidiary of Trinity Broadcasting Network

2442 Michelle Drive Tustin, CA 92780

Rights Department, 2442 Michelle Drive, Tustin, CA 92780.

Trilogy Christian Publishing/TBN and colophon are trademarks of Trinity Broadcasting Network.

For information about special discounts for bulk purchases, please contact Trilogy Christian Publishing.

Manufactured in the United States of America

10 9 8 7 6 5 4 3 2 1

Library of Congress Cataloging-in-Publication Data is available.

ISBN: 978-1-63769-788-7

E-ISBN: 978-1-63769-789-4

This book is a collaboration between many writers, each bringing their unique perspective.

Dedication

For Carolyn, who continually demonstrated her
unconditional love and support for me. I love you, Mom.

Acknowledgments

Our stories never end. We are continuously writing new chapters. My deepest gratitude goes out to everyone who participated in this project.

To those whose stories you've read, who so graciously shared with us some of the most vulnerable parts of themselves. Some are old friends, and some are new ones; we are all connected by our adoption journeys! Thank you!

To my husband and family for their love and support through this project. I love you!

To my friends, who are always cheering me on! You are the best!

To you, dear reader, thank you for picking up this book and embracing our stories. May they be a blessing to you and give you hope wherever you may be in your journey.

Much love,

Rosanne

Table of Contents

Surrender

The gift of life for you
Overwhelming joy and tears so real
A gift to me—daughters

One held close only in heart and prayer
I was merely a child then
Taking comfort knowing your mom held you
Strangers, yet, destined to meet
A perfect plan for both our lives
Shame erased, love takes its place

One I held your whole life through
Tears of joy, love at first sight
We know each other oh so well
Imperfect though it may be
Love so deep, forever true
Laughter and sorrow mark the days
Time passes in a blink

The past no more, no judgment here
Each day a precious gift
Now, I surrender all for love

RML 03-2020

Introduction

Every one of us has a unique story. I love hearing other people's stories. There's so much we can learn from each other when we listen with genuine curiosity. Honestly, I never thought I'd write a book. So, how did we arrive here? That part of my story involves meeting a stranger in a coffee shop in 2011. I'm out with a friend; we're enjoying lunch and catching up on each other's lives when a man walks over to us. He knew things no one could've known about us. Things he couldn't have overheard because these were not topics of our conversation. My friend doesn't recall anything he said to her, but I never forgot he told me I would write a book. The man confessed that sometimes the Holy Spirit moves him to speak to people, and he obediently speaks the words he's given. I felt confused at the time, and my only thought was, clearly, he's wrong because I'm not a writer. So, I dismissed the encounter as nothing more than him looking for someone to talk to.

The idea that I would write a book is the only part of the conversation I remember clearly and one that came to mind many times over the years. Now, I realize this was indeed the Holy Spirit speaking through him to plant a seed that's been germinating for nearly ten years. My biggest question remained year after year; what am I supposed to write about? I considered my interests and hobbies as possible subjects, but nothing felt right. Now, as unexpectedly as my encounter with that stranger, the answer presented itself. The story inside me, one I'd hidden away in shame for so long, was ready to come into the light. God has His way, and it's all in His timing.

These beautiful stories of adoption are shared from friends I've made in the past ten years and new friends I've gained since this project began. To all of us, God was guiding our paths to cross. If it were not for the intervening years and how I lived them, I would not be fulfilling this part of my story, the story God wrote for me before I was born.

A few months ago, I was asked to record a video testimony about my *Comeback* for my church's Easter Service (2021). When I first read the email, I came close to deleting it. No way was I going to have my face and story on the big screen at church. I know way too many people who will see it. Then, of course, I realized that's exactly what I need to do. Be obedient and be sure lots of people see and hear my story. God freed my voice, and He's using it to bless those I know and those I'll never know. Yes, it was scary and a little embarrassing. It was also amazing! And beautifully received and acknowledged by so many friends. Nearly all of whom knew nothing about this part of my story.

Adoption, I've come to realize, is an act of love to be celebrated, not one to be hidden in shame. As you journey with us through this book, you will see how God has orchestrated our stories for good in His perfect timing.

Since talking to the people who've contributed to this book and learning their stories, I find myself emotionally invested in their lives. My gratitude to each of them is sincere and deeply heartfelt. None of this would have been possible without their openness to share the most vulnerable parts of themselves. We will always have a connection to each other. Although I have not yet met them all in person or even on a phone call, I cherish each one as a friend.

One important lesson I've learned throughout this experience is to embrace every part of your story because it is God's story through you. Find someone you trust and love and share your joy and your pain. God uses it all for His glory. You just never know what incredible plan God has waiting for you when you trust Him. His hand is directing your story, too, whether you know it today or not yet.

By sharing our stories, I desire that you will find hope and freedom in the possibilities of restoration and reunion in your life. If you are not someone who has personal experience with adoption, perhaps you'll find more compassion for those of us on all sides of that story.

"For I know the plans I have for you, declares the Lord, plans to prosper you and not to harm you, plans to give you hope and a future" (Jeremiah 29:11).

"You are the God who performs Miracles; You display your power among the peoples" (Psalm 77:14).

"The greatest gift you can give other people is your story" (Judd Apatow).

Andrew

Andrew was introduced to me by a mutual friend. I was sharing my vision for this book with her and my realization that I needed men willing to tell their stories. It took her only a moment to say, "You have got to talk with Andrew; he has an incredible story."

We spoke on the phone, and this young man was so open and honest about his story. So willing to share how God is working in his life. I feel so strongly about hearing men's voices telling their story because again and again, I encountered people who knew men that were adopted but would absolutely never talk about their experience. This book would be incomplete without a diversity of voices. I am so grateful Andrew is willing to share his story with me and all of you!

Andrew's Story

When I was three days old, I was adopted promptly on my dad's birthday. What a birthday present that must have been! I remember hearing the story about how everyone in my family was so excited to meet me that they hosted a huge party at my parents' house. Even our church's lead pastor was there. My parents would later tell me that they could never have kids, and so they went the adoption route. "What a blessing your adoption was!" they would say all of the time. It wasn't until I was older that I realized how

17

much of a blessing adoption was for me.

My parents were open about my adoption as I grew up. It took me a while to truly understand what it meant when my mom would say she wasn't the one that gave birth to me. Truthfully, I didn't think much about it. When I became a teenager, I started making videos and communicating with my birth mom Laura. We would send things back and forth during the holidays and letters during the year. When I became a little older, we became friends on Facebook so we could keep up with each other's lives. Looking back on it now, I can only imagine what went through her mind when she would get things from me but hadn't met me, her only son. The rule my parents made was, "You can meet her any time after you turn eighteen."

Let's put a pause on my adoption story for a moment and give you a little back story on my faith journey.

I grew up in a Baptist church in the small town of Columbia, Illinois. Every Sunday, Mom and Dad would wake me up and dress me in my Sunday best. We would go to church and listen to Brother Don and later Pastor Jonathan preach, then we would go out to eat much as church families do. Sunday school was a staple, and of course, Wednesday night youth group too. Around eight or nine, I had the conversation with my parents that I believed in Jesus, and just like that, I took the plunge on a Sunday morning.

As I got older, I started to stray away from our youth group, and Sunday mornings became a burden, not something I wanted to be a part of. In high school, I focused on sports and friendships and less and less on Jesus. I'll never forget our Sunday graduation at church. Lonnie, our youth pastor, looked each one of us straight in the eye and said, "As you go off to college, get connected to ministry within the first couple of weeks, or you won't at all." Guess who turned down those words of advice. Yours truly.

My college experience (in Springfield, Missouri) fits well with what you might see in the movie *Animal House*. I spent a lot of time partying during my freshman year. Don't get me wrong, I love the friends I made, and some of the ridiculous memories we made will last forever, but there was definitely something missing. I remember when I would come back from college to visit family, the last thing I wanted to do was go to church. It's as if I felt embarrassed or ashamed to step foot in the church.

Fast forward to the summer between my junior and senior years of college. A good friend of mine had a party to celebrate his twenty-first birthday. In my mind, I thought it would be a good idea to snort some pills and drink until I couldn't stand up straight. The next morning, I woke up and decided it would be an even better idea not to eat or drink anything because I felt so bad. I spent most of the morning in the restroom (I'll spare you the details). Because I didn't hydrate at all, and with the combination of the pills, the alcohol, the lack of hydration, and being sick all morning, my body began to lock up. I was so dehydrated that my body started a process of shutting down. Luckily, a good friend of mine heard my cry and got me to the hospital. I remember telling him not to call my mom, which of course, he did. Thanks, Derek.

On that drive to the hospital, I began to experience a meltdown which I would later find out was a panic attack. I thought I was dying! At the ER, I laid in the bed as the doctor told me my body was shutting down due to dehydration. My parents had shown up at this point. I later found out my dad and sister were in a movie, and when my mom got the call, she went to the theater and was running through each room yelling to find them. I can only imagine how fast they drove down to Springfield. The doctor gave me multiple bags of fluids to get my body back to normal.

What is so unique about this day is that in those moments, I realized I wasn't invincible. I spent a huge portion of my senior year with a ton of anxiety. The fear of the next panic attack, fear of sickness, and ultimately for the first time, the fear of death overwhelmed me. My energy, my upbeat personality, and my happy-go-lucky style were no longer. One evening as I sat in my office at work, I had a thought that had never crossed my mind: *Why am I even here? What is the point of all of this?* I called my mom that evening but hung up and never told her why I even called. I was lost. I was confused. I was overwhelmed, and I didn't know where to turn. At one point, suicide even crossed my mind. Then, one of the most important moments of my life happened: I met my birth mom, Laura.

My dad and I are diehard Saint Louis Blues fans. It's one of the things that connects us at the hip. Any opportunity we have, we watch games together. You know it's bad when we have the Blue note tattooed on our arms! We were down in Nashville in March of my senior year to see the Blues play the Predators. A couple of our friends couldn't make the game, so we had to stand outside the arena to sell the extra tickets. Had we not had to sell those tickets, what happened next would have never come to be.

As we stood outside the arena, my phone vibrated. I pulled it out of my pocket. "To your left." I will *never* forget those words. They were from my birth mom Laura. The woman I had never met in my life. The one who unselfishly gave me up after she held me in her arms. The same woman who selflessly spent the past twenty-two years of her life watching my life from a far. I can't even fathom the emotions she had gone through over the last twenty-two years, and now here I was, standing right down the street from her. She saw the back of my head from blocks away and knew it was me, and yet instead of running to me, she left it up to me.

I looked up at my dad and showed him the message. He looked over my shoulder. "She's right there," he said. A million thoughts raced through my mind at this moment. *Do I turn around and make eye contact? Do I walk into the arena? Do I completely ignore all of it?* "What do I do?" I asked him. My dad's response was simple and perfect, "It's up to you."

I turned and made eye contact with my birth mom for the first time. The world slowed down around me, and I don't really remember the next few minutes very well. I

21

remembered walking towards her, tears streaming down her face, and then an embrace that lasted for what seemed like hours. To be honest, I didn't know what to think or what to feel in these first moments meeting my birth mom. After we separated, we decided to meet at the hotel after the game. Let's just say I don't remember the game at all.

When we got back to the hotel, we sat in the lobby with her husband and my dad for a couple of hours, talking about anything and everything. Laura discussed how my life would not be near what it was had she kept me. Her struggles with job consistency, relationships, and so many other things would have impacted who I was as a child. It was in these moments I started to realize how blessed I was. God is real. He has a plan, He's kept me going some- how for the last year, and now He's set in motion my one- hundred-and-eighty-degree turn.

We got back to Columbia the next day, and I headed back to college. I'll never forget that as I crossed the bridge into Missouri, I broke down. I was overwhelmed by the sit- uation and by what God had done for me. The Holy Spirit filled my car. Tears streaming down my face, I turned the car around and headed back home. I ran downstairs to the basement where my parents were and cried a cry unlike any before. I had been hurting for the better part of a year, and this moment felt like the beginning of a massive change in my life.

My senior year finished up, and I went down south to Houston, Texas, for an internship at Houston's first Baptist church. My cousin had hooked me up with this internship, and I said yes for Lord knows what reason. I hadn't been to church or practiced religion in years, and I still, to this day, don't know why I said yes. The management there had me take charge of a bunch of God-fearing, Jesus-loving high school and college students. Isn't that comical? God was probably sitting up on His throne, getting a mighty chuckle out of this situation.

The weekend before the camp started, we had a retreat to get the staff together and connect with one another and Jesus. I'll never forget that Sunday morning. As the counselors and high school students stood around worshipping, I lost it. Everything that had happened to me over the last year and beyond was building up to that moment, on that couch, in the middle of a small town in Texas. It was in those few minutes I realized what I had been missing in my life—Jesus Christ. But here's the beauty, He was with me the whole time; I just didn't notice.

The life change I experienced at twenty-two will be something I will always remember. Anxiety and depression turned into joy and anticipation. My life was back on track. All of these moments would have never happened in my life had it not been for a selfless act by a beautiful woman and a perfect plan set in motion by God. Adoption, what a picture of love and grace. I was adopted into a family, much like God adopts us into His family.

I am the son of Brian and Sharon Thompson, I am the son of Laura Merryman, and I am a child of God.

Sharon

My phone conversation with Sharon was one I was especially looking forward to because I have not yet had an opportunity to talk with my daughter's adoptive mom. Sharon was open and shared her family's story freely and with love. Personally, it's comforting to me to understand better how she felt; how she and Andrew's birth mom have grown their relationship. I am inspired that one day (hopefully soon!) I can create an affirming relationship with my daughter's mom. Meeting face-to-face in 2020 (during COVID-19) just wasn't a possibility. Sharon has been so graciously supportive of my desire for this conversation, and I appreciate her insights!

Sharon's Story, Adoptive Mom

My husband Brian and I were trying to have kids, and that wasn't meant to be. So, we prayed about it a lot and started searching out the adoption option. Initially, we applied to several organizations just to get a feeling for what they wanted and to learn how the process worked. This was thirty-one years ago when we first started. It was almost twenty-nine years ago when we adopted our son, Andrew, so it was quite different than today. We were getting information from some agencies, and one (I wish I would have kept the paper) had the cost divided up where if you want a baby in three months, it costs this much; if you want a baby in six months, it costs this much. Brian and I looked at each other, and we thought, *Oh no! This is not meant for us.* This felt like we were buying a baby, which is not right. We continue to pray, and then we checked out Bethany Christian Services. That's when everything clicked. They did not have a social worker for the Southern Illinois area at that time, so they had to contract with a freelance person. She came to the house and talked with us, and later, we met with her at a church and had to go through the process for the adoption agency. Asking us questions to see if we were even eligible to adopt children. I was too young at the time, and my husband Brian is six years older than I am. We had to wait two years until I turned twenty-five before we could begin the process so, that was a little bit of an issue. We felt like God led us to Bethany; actually, we know for a fact that He did.

We went through the agency, and their typical waiting list was anywhere from a year to a year and a half for the adoption of an infant to go through. We were the longest one at the time. We were probably two and a half years. We had to create our profile: a booklet about ourselves, our family, and our beliefs so that birth mothers and birth fathers could look at it. At this point, our information was still anonymous. We got a call the day before Easter that someone picked us out. We didn't know anything about them. And we did not meet them beforehand. But when he was born, we went to the hospital.

That's when we got to meet Laura and her family. She was holding him. We were sitting there thinking, *Oh my gosh! This is so amazing!* We weren't adopting him at this point. We were just meeting him for the first time. Laura could have changed her mind; she might not have liked us. She could have just said, "Oh no, they're all wrong." More than anything, we wanted to hold him, but we were going to let her bring him to us first. We sat and talked for a while, and then Laura said, "Do you want to hold him?" Oh, my goodness! I think we were both crying, of course, we did! He was such a precious little thing. This all took place in Chicago, Illinois.

We went back to the hotel and waited for a couple of days. Brian had always said that his best birthday present would be adopting a baby on his birthday. Andrew was born on April 21; that's the day we met him and Laura. He was placed with us on April 24, which is Brian's birthday. We had this realization, *Okay, God, we understand. He is a gift from You. We hear You; we understand You. This is the day we were supposed to adopt him.* We got a call from the social worker for Laura, his birth mother, and she said, "You're supposed to be here at this time today. But we're going to postpone it a little bit because Laura is having trouble. We're not going to go in and make her sign something while she's upset." Of course, everyone's upset at that point. We worried maybe this isn't going to go through. I remember getting in the shower and just crying out to God. "We don't want to take this little boy away from his birth mom if we're not supposed to." It was a long couple of hours, but she did sign. We went back to the hospital. When we had the placement, both of our parents were there with us. They got to make the trip. And it was absolutely amazing! It was awfully hard to see Laura so visibly upset, and

we tried to reassure her that we're going to do everything
in our power to bring him up in a godly home, and he will
always know you and those kinds of things.

Our contact with Laura after the adoption was all
pre-arranged as far as how much contact we would have.
I don't remember the specifics. At that time, you had to
develop film and actually had photos. I was always taking
pictures. I'd get doubles of everything and send her a whole
pack of pictures with a letter. Updates about what he was
doing, how he was fitting in the family, and how everyone
loves him. How when we take him to church, everybody's
just *ooh-ing* and *ahh-ing* over him. After maybe three or
four years of corresponding with Laura, there was a space
of time where we didn't communicate. Then, God started
putting in my mind that I needed to reach out to Laura. This
was when we got a call from Bethany saying that Laura
was wanting to reach out to us to see if we could start communication again. And of course, we said yes. It may have
been at that time when we started making VHS tapes and
sending them to her. I think that was just a godsend for her
to get more information about Andrew. I guess we stopped
because we had agreed that we were going to keep in communication for the first couple of years. I think we did more
than what we had agreed.

We just kept the communication going after reconnecting this time. Laura did lose quite a few years where she
didn't hear anything. I feel bad about that now because I
know that probably would have really helped her. We never
had any hesitation about communicating with Laura. I just

thought this is the least we can do after what she did for us and Andrew. I was more than happy to do that, and so was my husband. We were always on the same page, so to speak, of keeping her informed and just trying to ease any kind of pain she might be feeling, even a little bit, by letting her know that he's thriving; he's amazing; he's a gift from God. We will never ever be able to thank her enough. It was always a positive experience. I know Laura was very appreciative and thankful. When she would write back or sent him something, she was overly generous. Generous to the point where she was even thinking of Rebecca, Andrew's younger sister, our (adopted) daughter. Laura always included her, which was, I thought, just very telling of her heart. She is a special person.

Andrew always knew that he was adopted. He knew that Laura was his birth mom. There wasn't a time we sat him down and said, "We have something to tell you." We would show him pictures of Laura and naturally say, "This is your birth mother." He didn't understand when he was very young. I remember him at some point saying something about "When I was in your belly," and I said, "You weren't in my belly, you were in Laura's belly. Remember Laura?" and I'd show him a picture. So, it started when he was young, and it was just a natural part of the conversation. We'd give Andrew information that was appropriate for his age. We were incredibly open about it and talked about it all the time. There were times when you're getting everybody ready, and you're trying to get out the door, and all of a sudden, he said something (I don't remember what it was), but we all stopped in our tracks. "Okay, we need to talk about this right now."

He didn't have face-to-face contact with Laura until he was in college. When he began to have more of a relationship with her, it was good. I had no problems, no concerns. It's honestly just never been an issue. Again, I think I owe a lot of that to Laura because she's always been open and inclusive, including me in things. She was open about how she did not want to come in as a mother figure; she "just wanted to be his friend," is how she put it; she just wanted to be involved in his life, being able to see him occasionally. We really hit it off, Laura and me.

It seemed we were more like sisters, so there was no jealousy, no bad feelings. When Andrew called me that night, he said, "Mom, I've got something big to tell you when I get home tomorrow." I knew immediately what it was. I just had a feeling. I didn't want to say to him that I thought I knew because I wanted him to tell me when he could. I was thrilled for him and her because I knew it had been a long hard journey for her. She deserved to know Andrew.

I want everyone to think about how you're blessing the birth mother and birth father and the birth family by keeping in touch so they know how that child is doing. They are our kids, both of them. There's never been a second where we doubted anything that we've done. I feel certain God placed them with us. I don't know how else to describe it. I can't imagine our life without them, and I cannot imagine loving them more had I given birth to them.

Laura

Connecting with Laura was like reuniting with an old friend. Our first phone call lasted over two hours. Much of the time, we talked about life in general, just getting to know each other. We started with one thing in common (both being birth moms) and, during our conversation, realized how much alike we are and how many similar life experiences we share. Our conversation went far beyond our children. This was the first real conversation I've ever had with another birth mom, with someone who went through what I did. I am so grateful for her willingness to share her story and more so for her friendship!

Laura's Story, Birth Mom

I got pregnant at sixteen, and Andrew's birth father, Eric, was a freshman in college. Eric was being influenced by his mom and dad to end our relationship. They said they would no longer help with tuition and would take away his car. He made his choice; he listened to his parents. I was really upset with him, knowing I was not going to get any support from him or his family with whatever decision I was going to make.

Not long after Eric and I broke up, I met my first real

boyfriend. He was stationed at Great Lakes Naval Training Center in Chicago. We were engaged to be married when Andrew was born. He was with me at the hospital the whole time I was in labor with Andrew. Everyone thought he was Andrew's father. Eric came to the hospital for an hour when Andrew was born. Andrew and I were together in the hospital for seventy-two hours before I had to sign the papers to relinquish him so he could be adopted. I couldn't sign those papers! I talked with my parents and my fiancé's mother. They kept saying I can't give him what he needs, I can't do this, even though I was getting married to someone else.

Everything was so messed up, and I just did not want to sign those papers at all, but I felt like I was pressured into signing. So, I did. I didn't know that you had up to six months to change your mind. In hindsight, I'm glad I didn't know that because I probably would have tried to get him back. That was the worst day of my life. The way it was set up with family services, for the first two years, his parents would keep in contact with me through the adoption agency. I always got letters and pictures of him. Andrew's parents were good enough and nice enough to keep in contact with me. They didn't have to. And then when I turned thirty, I found out I couldn't have any more children. I realized Andrew was going to be my only child, so I contacted the adoption agency, and they contacted his parents. Andrew's parents freely gave me their contact information and said, "If you want to, send everything to us." That's when I got his last name and address. After that, everything

I did, letters, presents for birthday and Christmas, we directly communicated with each other. Andrew and I would email each other. We never talked on the phone, and then, the next thing was social media, but we still never talked on the phone. I left it up to him. I believe you don't want to pressure your child that you gave up for adoption to have a relationship with you.

I'd send him an email or message and say, "Hey, if you ever want to talk to me, here's my number, don't forget I'm always here. You can call me and talk to me anytime you want." I left that open for him. It was when you're ready because I didn't want to do that to him or his parents that adopted him.

I know he told you the story about how we first met in person. This is the way I saw it. My niece was here from Texas, and everybody wants to go downtown when they come to visit Nashville. I knew he was a Saint Louis Blues hockey fan. I also knew he was going to Nashville Predators games when the Blues would play here because he would email me and talk to me about this stuff. So, we were walking downtown with my niece, and I had no idea that Blues were playing the Predators that night.

When I realized there was a game, I sent him a message asking, "Are you here watching the Blues playing?" His response was, "Yes, we're bar-hopping." We were in a store nearby, and I told my husband, "I have got to go over there." "There are thousands of people over there," he said. I said, "I don't care. I know I'm probably not going to see him. I only know that I must go over there."

We were standing far away, and I saw the back of his head, and I just knew it was him. I knew it was him! I don't know why or how I knew because it was just the back of his head. I said to my husband, "I know that's my son." We walked closer, and when I saw his face, I turned my back towards him. My husband was still facing him. I sent a message and said, "Look to your left." To my husband, I asked, "What's going on?" He was talking to his Dad. Then the next thing I knew, he's walking toward us.

I could have walked over there, and he could have just walked away, and that would have been horrible. So, I took a really big chance because if he wouldn't have responded or if he didn't walk towards me, I was going to walk away myself. As a birth mother, I think it's the appropriate thing to do. I don't know if there are a lot of mothers out there who would be able to do that. I think some would. I just never wanted to overstep my boundaries.

He said, "I'll text you and tell you what we're doing after the game, and we can meet up." My phone's going dead in the meantime, because I'm calling everybody, so I gave him my husband's number. He sent a message, "Hey, we're going back to the hotel. Do you want to meet us in the hotel lobby?" Yes! We all went over there, my husband and my sister, my niece, and her husband. We talked, and I told him that I love him; I thought about him every single day, and I gave him up because I could not give him the life he deserves. I was honest about it; I just couldn't do it. After we left the hotel, this is when all the nerves start coming. I'm driving home thinking, *Is that the first and last time I'll ever see him? What if he doesn't want to see me again? What if he doesn't want to talk to me?*

I was nervous, and I was crying because I just didn't know how to feel. A couple of days later, he texted me a picture, and he'd shaved his head. I felt such relief when I received that message because I didn't want to reach out to him. I waited for him to reach out to me. *Thank you, God,* I thought, *he still wants something to do with me.*

My mom and stepdad were married when I gave him up, so, of course, they wanted to meet Andrew. The four of us went for a visit (we live about four hours' drive from where he lives). At this time, I still had not talked to his mother. She did not want to talk to me on the phone until she met me. We arrived on a Friday, and all went over to their house. When I saw his mother, I hugged her and didn't want to let go of her either. We spent the day together and just talked. It turned out, the next day, they had planned a family reunion. I felt overwhelmed because all his aunts and uncles, Grandpa and Grandma, and his cousins were there. I was so nervous.

Everybody was so sweet. When I walked in the door, they kept saying "Thank you" repeatedly. At first, I couldn't understand why; then, I saw their point of view. I understand now. They all wrote me these beautiful letters. Most said, in their own way, "Thank you for giving us Andrew." I treasure these letters and will always keep them. Since then, Andrew and I visit several times a year. His mom and I are so much alike; we have so much in common, what we do and how we act. I think it's strange because they're the parents I chose for Andrew. They are the parents that my son was meant to grow up with. I don't know how, but that's what was supposed to happen. The night before we met all of Andrew's family at that reunion, his mom gifted me a necklace she made. It had two white pearls and one blue one; the two white ones were representing me and her, and the blue one for Andrew.

That's when I said to all of them, "I want you to know that I'm not stepping in here wanting to be Andrew's mother, I know I gave birth to him, but I'm not really his mother."

I wanted them to understand that because I didn't want his parents, especially his mom, to feel threatened or hurt because I was in Andrew's life again. Honestly, I only want to be his friend. I don't want to take that mother role. I gave up that privilege seventy-two hours after I gave birth to him.

I knew Andrew's birth father, Eric, was a good guy, and I wasn't expecting anything to be wrong, but I wanted to do a background check just to make sure before I gave Andrew his information. When I did the background check on his dad, everything was good. I found he still had a home phone, so I called, and I left a message saying, "Hey, this is a friend from high school. I just wanted to touch base with you and see how you're doing." I didn't know where his birth father was as far as his situation; whether he was married or had kids. He recognized my voice, and he thought

Andrew might need a kidney or something. So, when he called me, I told him what happened. And he said that he would love to talk to Andrew, and I said, "Okay, I will give him your number." Well, not too long after that, I talked to his birth father again. He's married and has two kids, and his wife is not on board at all with the situation; she wants nothing to do with it. And Eric said to me, "I want to talk to him; I want to meet him someday." I think Andrew, knowing how his birth father's wife feels about it, hasn't contacted him because he doesn't want to interrupt that life. If Eric's wife were on board with it, I think Andrew would have called him by now, but she's just not ready. Maybe things will change one day. Every time I see Andrew, I ask if he's talked to his birth father, and he says no. He may call him at some point, or he may have already talked to him, and I just don't know about it.

Andrew has been able to come here every summer, usually in July, and then we usually go there once a year. My mom and I went up there last year (2020). We see each other at least twice a year. If his parents are coming through town on their way to visit Andrew's sister, their adopted daughter in Georgia, they'll call me, and we'll meet them for lunch, so we stay in contact consistently. I talk to his mother probably more than him. She has a close relationship with Andrew.

Andrew and I, we're just really good friends. I had an automatic connection with Andrew from the beginning. It was so natural. He and I are so much alike. He acts just like I do; his personality is just like mine. I'll always remember the first time he called me "Mom." Usually, he would just introduce me as his birth mother. That's how it was for several years. When Andrew introduced me to someone and said, "This is my mom," my heart soared! I thought, *Wow, I have someone to call me mom.* I've never had that; I never had any kids after him. He's now met most of my close family, my sisters, and brothers, my nieces. For my 40th birthday, all I asked was for Andrew and his parents to be there for my party.

At the party, Andrew and I were sitting next to each other, and even though my step-kids were sitting rather far away, they said, "Oh my God, he's just like her," so everybody can see those similarities. Because I didn't raise him, I wondered how he could take after me with that kind of stuff. I understand now, some of your behaviors and certain personality traits are genetic, and some come from the way you were brought up. I'm continually amazed that we are so much alike. There are a lot of things that he gets from his birth father, like being an athlete. His height comes from his dad, too. Andrew and my brother share physical traits too. I have a picture of the two of them side by side. Oh my God. Everyone says we look alike; I don't really see that, but I guess we do.

I know Andrew says that we met each other at the right time because he was going down the wrong path in life, a destructive path as I had done.

Andrew and I had the same upbringing as far as growing up in the church. As a young person, I was in the church at least four days a week; I was in Calvinists, which was like the Brownies (Girl Scouts) for the church. I was in the church choir. My family was deacons and elders in the church, and that's the way I was brought up. Sadly, my church turned its back on me when I got pregnant. That's why I fell away from the church. I can say I didn't stop believing at first, but it was extremely hard, and I had a very rough life.

I felt like I could not give him a good life. When I was a teenager, my father committed suicide, and my life drastically changed. We were that family that went to church all the time, that white-picket-fence family. My family was going through a lot. I just did not want to raise Andrew in the circumstances around me at the time. I didn't think it was right. I wanted him to have a better life, a life I knew I could not provide for him. Some people thought I was being selfish by giving him up and not keeping him. Now when I look back, that's not what it was. I was not being selfish. I was giving him to a family that really could take care of him and give him a great life, a great future.

After Andrew was born, I lived in eleven different states. I was all over the place. I was so bitter towards everything; my life was messed up for so many years. It took me until I was in my 30s to get my life together. I'm grateful that it didn't take Andrew that long because it's no fun. It's hard. And there were days I decided I wasn't going to make it. Andrew said he was having suicidal thoughts but did not act on them. I actually tried. I didn't succeed, obviously, but I've been hospitalized several times because

I did try. That's just being honest. I was in such an awful place that I didn't want to live. I didn't feel like there was any purpose. I was constantly trying to get out of things, just not be around. I always thought everyone else would be better without me.

I had my hysterectomy when I was thirty, and after that, I was so mad at God. I pleaded with God, "Why would You do this to me when I gave my only child up for adoption? And now, I can't have any more kids! What did I do that was so bad?" I blamed Him for everything. I had no relationship with God at that point; I could say I stopped believing. Now it's different. Everything in my life has changed. Many things changed before I met Andrew, thank God. My husband really helped me get my life together. It took me to decide to do it, but he did help me. When I met my son, I finally realized why God made me wait. I'm going to be honest with you; I was a mess for several years. God was waiting.

He was waiting for me to get my life together, to have a good husband and a good life before I met Andrew. And that's what happened.

When we met, I did not know that Andrew was in such a bad place. There were things he went through that I didn't find out until last year or the year before. My and Andrew's paths were similar, although his path was shorter than mine. Andrew was speaking on adoption at a conference, so my mom and I and his mom and grandmother attended. And that's the first time I ever heard about the pills he took, but

I didn't say anything. He's always incredibly open about what he went through. I don't know what made him go on the straight and narrow. Meeting me helped Andrew realize that he was really blessed, and God was real and had a plan. His job in Houston also led him to truly find God, and he turned his life around.

He's had a good life. I've shared with him that he probably wouldn't have had a great life with me. He looked back too, and that's when he decided to change his ways as well. So, that is a big, big part of both of our lives.

Today, when I look back on all those years that I was angry and wondering why I can't meet my son, I know it was not the right time. I am thankful that Andrew didn't come back into my life before that because I wouldn't have wanted him to see all that stuff. That was truly a blessing from God. How my life has changed. I know everything happened for a reason. It seemed as though God was saying, "Okay, it's your turn. You got this. You're in a good place now. Let's go. Let's do this." I've stopped being angry with God. After I met Andrew, all that bitterness and being angry at life in general just went away. Finally, I knew why I'd never met him before.

1. Laura holding Andrew with Sharon and Brian
2. Family photo: Andrew, his sister Rebecca, Sharon and Brian
3. Andrew, Sharon and Laura
4. Laura and Andrew

Monica

I was introduced to Monica through one of her family members. Both of whom were strangers to me before this project began. Monica's story is one of longing and of feeling like there's a missing piece in her life, not unlike how many adoptees feel. Her reunion with her birth family is fairly recent, and they are all still figuring out how to navigate it.

Monica asked her birth sister to share her story, which follows Monica's here. Due to family circumstances, this sibling has asked to remain anonymous as some of the other siblings have not welcomed Monica into the family as openly as she has done. One day, I hope to meet Monica's sister. I appreciate her willingness to share.

Monica's Story

My name is Monica, I was born January 23, 1976, and I met my parents a few days later. I had a normal childhood; I played with my dolls, played sports, sang, and had lots of friends. My parents divorced when I was quite young, they both remarried, and my father had two more girls, my little sisters. I have always known I was adopted. My Mom used to tell me I was handpicked, that I was so special because two mommies loved me!

As I got older, I started to wonder why I didn't feel

like I fit in. I can't put my finger on why I felt like that, but something just seemed to be missing. I was loved, had friends, and had so many activities; there was just something missing. You know, when you forget to add something to a cake, like salt, and it still looks great, but when you bite in, it just isn't the same? That's what the feeling was; it could've been better, but it was already pretty great. As a teenager, I was going through so many emotions and new things trying to find my way in the world. So, when I was eighteen, I decided to find my birth family, knowing little bits and pieces from my mother like my birth family lived in a rural area; they were married and had other children before me. I searched for a bit but could not find anything too helpful, so I let it go.

Life happened. I moved and traveled, got married, and had kids of my own. And still had a *missing something* feeling. I got divorced and continued to raise babies. And still, many years later, I could not figure it out. Fast forward to close to my 40th birthday, I had been taking care of my mother with dementia, getting ready to marry for the second time, and struggling with my connection with my daughters.

I was still searching. I had prayed throughout the years, wondering if I would have regrets if I decided to find the family I knew I had. It was clear I needed to find them. I grew up in the church, went to more 6 a.m. masses than I could count with my grandmother Martina. When I was about seventeen, she and I had a conversation that stuck with me over the years even after she was gone. She was someone I confided in, my rock when I felt I had no one. She told me that no matter what I found, I had a loving and understanding family. So, it was time. And I believe He (God) had a hand in it.

After I married my wife, we decided to go out of the country, and I needed my birth certificate. See, that birth certificate had never moved from the place my mom had it; every time I needed it, there it was in the same spot. It wasn't this time. I saw my chance to get my information, and so I did. You must have a notary sign-off for the *real* (original) birth certificate. My wife drove up to Topeka and hand-delivered my request, and retrieved a copy of my other birth certificate for the moment.

When the letter arrived some weeks later, I knew what it contained. I left the envelope sitting unopened for several days and then several more open but unread. It was an official letter from Topeka, and I didn't want to open it. What if they didn't have a record of it? What if they did, but I was too late to find my family? What if, what if, what if? I finally opened it and found the names of a married couple. I waited with that information and looked at it several times over the next week or so. I finally started to search the internet for the names that were in front of me. It was a process that was overwhelming and peaceful at the same time.

I was finding information on people and making a list of where to look. I came across an obituary, and the names of pallbearers looked familiar. It was my brother, at least that's what I thought; I found him on Facebook and was set to reach out to him. Then, a friend I had confided in about all of this stopped me. She told me to call my (birth) mother, and I appreciate that advice now because, at the time, their kids did not know.

I was at work after a long day, and I just called; it was right before the holidays, and I had just lost my mother less than a year prior, and I was searching, searching for understanding, or so I thought. I was so nervous, and no, not in a good way, my doubts came flooding in as I picked up the phone and dialed. I called the home number listed. I had rehearsed this so many times over the years, and all I could get out was, "Did you give a baby up for adoption on January 23, 1976?" Tears were already flowing, and this woman on the other end of the phone excused herself for a second. I knew this was her; I knew I had found her, but what was she going to say? Those moments of waiting seemed like my entire life. She covered the phone and spoke to someone, telling them to have a good time and she would see them later. She then walked somewhere and shut a door.

"I did not think it would have taken so long for you to find me," she said. Relief. We spent an hour on the phone that day, lots of tears and more laughter. She took me on her journey, and although I had given it up to God a long time ago, I had some answers. The timing was right to have spoken to her that day, relief was great, but I still did have a lot of questions on things that we didn't talk about. I was in shock that night when I got home, dinner was cold because I had planned on being home in twenty minutes, not an hour, but my wife asked me all the right questions, neither of us cared. We warmed up dinner, and I relived the conversation over again.

My mom and I met in person a month later, she was coming through town, and we met up in a gas station parking lot since I didn't know this lady from Eve. I saw her in her minivan, and I didn't see me. I thought for sure she would look just like me. But she seemed so familiar in other ways; we made our way to a coffee shop close by, sipped our tea and lemonade, and talked about her life and mine. I watched her, the nervousness and the mannerisms; there was our connection.

We spoke over the next couple of months, and I left it up to her whether she'd tell anyone about me. I was fine with whatever connections I could have with my birth family. She told her children at a sit-down restaurant at one of the grandkid's graduations. There are a lot of stories and memories from my siblings about that day, the day they found out about me. They apparently looked me up on Google and Facebook to see what I looked like as well; it was only right since I had done that to them months earlier.

I spoke to them on the phone, and two of the four siblings came to meet my daughter and me on Labor Day. We ate at a local place and just didn't want the day to end. We sat around and told stories. It's uncanny; the feeling of knowing people even if just meeting. How we interacted and the way we spoke were so similar.

We don't talk often enough, but it doesn't seem to matter how much time goes by; we are right back in as if no time has passed. My story is still being written. There were so many mixed emotions about finding family since I had a beautiful family all along, but I wouldn't change it. I don't feel that longing anymore.

Sibling's Story, Birth Sister

On May 21, 2016, my immediate family of six (Mom, Dad, and three siblings) would be changed forever. My mother had just broken the news to my siblings and me that we had another sister. It was an unusual setting for news of this nature to be communicated. It was at a restaurant after my niece's high school graduation. We had been eating, drinking, and laughing a ton; that is everyone but Mom. She was nervous, anxious, and just not herself. She kept saying, "Before anyone leaves, I need to talk to you kids." So, as we finished with dinner, all the grandkids, my sister-in-law, brothers-in-law, and my father, headed to the parking lot. My siblings and I stayed back to hear what Mom had to say. We were taken back because we had no idea what we were about to be told. Wow! Oh, wow, that is not what we expected to hear. "Another sister!" "What!?"

Mom said, "I had an affair. I am not sure if she is your father's daughter or this other man. Your father knows about her, but I was not able to keep her because I was told that I would lose the four of you. I couldn't bear that, so I gave her up for adoption. Oh, one more thing, don't mention this to your father because I haven't told him that she has contacted me." Again, the reaction was, "What!?"

Mom proceeded to tell us about their very first conversation. Sometime later, we realized that we were all at my brother's house celebrating Christmas when Mom received a call and seemed extremely shocked. Her face went blank and white then she immediately started to tear up. She walked into the other room, and when she returned, we could tell that she had been crying. We asked what the matter was, but she downplayed it and said that she was getting a migraine. As odd as that was, none of us pressed any further. Looking back to that night, I realized that Mom was happy, stressed, and upset from crying, but I feel she was relieved, too. She had found her daughter!

While we were talking to Mom, I was filled with a range of emotions. I was so confused about how something like this could have been kept secret for forty years. It was not only my mom's secret, but it was my dad's secret too. I felt cheated, shocked, mad about the situation and how it all happened. Mad that she was unable to grow up with us, but I was also happy and excited. I knew instantly that I wanted to meet her. What I didn't know was how my other siblings felt about having another sister. How was I going to navigate these waters and not cause family drama?

As we entered the parking lot from the restaurant, we said goodbye to Mom and Dad. As they drove away, the family swarmed around us. Here came all the grandkids, my sister-in-law, brothers-in-law, and my husband. They were all saying, "What did she want?" "What did she say?" We were all laughing and joking around about why she was being so dramatic, but no one, not one of them, guessed this. "You all will not believe this, but we have another sister!" "What!?" It was the same reaction we had. The bomb had just been dropped, a secret that had been kept for over forty years.

As my family (my husband and kids) left the restaurant parking lot and headed to my brother's house to spend the night, the conversation was about the news that we had just been told. My husband and kids were just as shocked as I was. I was no longer the baby of the family. With the snap of a finger, I now had three sisters (not just the two I grew up with) and one brother. We all joked that this was something you would see on a daytime talk show. It was complete craziness!

I could not wait to get back to my brother's house so we could talk to him about this. I desperately wanted to know more! I wanted to know what she looked like, what she was like, was she married, did she have kids, and so on.

My brother and I instantly looked her up on Google when we got back to the house. We were both so surprised by what we saw. She looked just like me. She was a cross between me and my oldest sister. It was astonishing! We continued our research and saw that she was married and that she had a daughter. Again, I was in complete awe because her daughter resembled my daughter. I couldn't wait to meet her.

As I returned home, I couldn't stop thinking about her and my family dynamics. I found myself overwhelmed and stressed, unsure what to do. I didn't want to cause waves in the family, but I knew I wanted to meet her. I talked to my brother, and he felt that same way. He reached out to her over the phone, and they set a time to meet. He called me and asked me if I would like to come, and we could meet her together.

On September 4, 2016, we met for the first time. We met at this quiet little Italian restaurant. Well, it was quiet until we got there. It was my brother with his family of four plus a friend of his youngest daughter, my family of four, and my newfound sister with her daughter. We laughed and joked and talked about our lives while we enjoyed the meal. After lunch was over, she invited us back to her house.

We picked up right where we left off. Zinging each other, laughing until we cried; lots and lots of conversation. We went outside and took pictures, and it is amazing how much we all resemble each other.

After spending several hours together, it was time to leave and head back home. My family headed to a nearby gas station, where we met up with my brother and his family. We were all in awe. "What did we just witness?" She had the same mannerisms, the same personality, and the same sense of humor. She was *us* but in a different shape and size. We were all blown away by the similarities even though she had grown up in a completely different family and had a completely different upbringing. It was apparent that we were related and not just related; we were *sisters*.

The more and more we are around each other, the more irritated I get about the situation; that she was not able to grow up with us, and we lost forty years together. I fully believe she is my father's daughter.

It has now been four and a half years since I found out about her and got to meet her. I still struggle with maintaining family peace since not all my siblings are as accepting of her as my brother and me. For me, I know I want to be able to share more of my life with her. I want to share holidays, special occasions, family gatherings, and so much more. I don't want to be divided as a family.

I know there is also a balance that we must manage between her adopted and biological families. I don't want to put additional pressure on her, but I know I want more. I want to be in her life more and want her in mine. I just don't fully know if that is what she wants, so I tend to shy away. I have realized when it comes to my family that I can only do what makes me happy, and I shouldn't worry about others. Easier said than done, but I am trying to work on this. I am just thankful I have her in my life now, and I don't want to lose any more time.

1. Monica with her parents
2. Monica and her birth sister
3. Monica and her birth family

Robyn

I have known Robyn for many years; however, I didn't know adoption was part of her story until a mutual friend shared that fact with me. When I spoke with Robyn, she was thrilled to share her story with us. As you will see, her reunion with her birth family looks a little bit different than she'd hoped. It is nonetheless beautiful and filled with joy.

I have not yet had the pleasure of meeting Sally or Beverly in person. They relayed their stories to me through Robyn. One day I hope we will have the opportunity to meet in person so I can express my deep gratitude to them for sharing with us.

Robyn's Story, Born on Christmas Day

Longer than I can remember, I have known I was adopted. I was born on Christmas Day, 1963. My parents brought me home on March 26, 1964. For the first three months of my life, I was in the hospital and foster care, where they called me Sunny. There are only two pictures of me from this time. My parents never kept my adoption a secret. From a young age, they would read me a bedtime story about an adopted family so that I would understand the concept of adoption. I learned from them that my biological parents made an exceedingly difficult and loving choice. They were too young to raise me when I was born and wanted me to have a good life. My parents (Bob and

Sally) longed to have children. They told me how much they loved me, and they chose me. When I was almost five years old, they adopted my brother. I still remember getting to see him before they did. When my parents saw him, my mom gasped, and he was put into her arms. I had a happy childhood.

Growing up, I sometimes wondered if my biological parents thought about me. Looking at the family picture wall in my grandparents' house, my brother and my pictures proudly displayed, I thought, *Who do I look like?* I loved the people on the wall but, I did not look like them. As I got older, I watched TV programs with long separated biological families meeting each other. I deeply wished that were me. I did not tell anyone of my desire. I did not look for my biological family; I understood that I might be a secret. A very big secret. I was told my biological parents probably did not stay together. They probably had separate families that did not know about me. I also did not want to hurt or disrespect my parents. I love them so much.

All through my school years, I knew other kids that were adopted. My friends all knew I was adopted. It was never an issue. I was happy to talk about it. It is just a part of who I am.

When I was fifteen, I met Gary. We met riding horses, I took riding lessons, and he owned a horse. He liked to show off jumping his horse when I was around. He first asked me out on a date when I was fifteen, but my parents would not allow me to date until I was sixteen. Fortunately, he asked

me out again when I was sixteen, and I went on my first
date with Gary. We dated for six or seven months. We dated
again one summer when he was home from college. And
then, when he graduated college, we started dating again
and have been together ever since. We married when I was
twenty-four years old. We have been married for thirty-two
years, and I love the life we have created for ourselves. We
have one adult son, Josh, that we adore. We moved around
the country for Gary's work and lived in many interesting
places making great friends. We have had fifteen different
addresses, to be exact. I cannot imagine life without Gary
and Josh. I am grateful, and I see God's hand in my life.
Everything had to happen the way it did to get me where I
am now.

I had little information about my biological parents
and heritage. The adoption agency provided my family
with one and a half pages of non-identifying information.
When DNA testing became available, I wanted to do it. In
2011, I took an Ancestry.com test to learn more about my
heritage. At first, the information from Ancestry.com was
not consistent with the little information I had. As more
people took the test, the more accurate the results became.
Later Ancestry.com started showing DNA matches. I had
lots of distant cousins, but no parental or sibling matches.
In March of 2015, I received a message from a third-fourth
cousin requesting my family tree information because he
was adopted and had no information. Unfortunately, I had
nothing for him.

A few years later, a fourth-sixth cousin contacted me.

My husband and I share an Ancestry.com account; she was looking at his tree, which did not make sense with the connection she had found to me. My husband explained to her that I was adopted, and I was born in California. She suggested that I look at a branch of the Glenn family that had moved to California during the Dust Bowl. Before I took the time to investigate that lead (not that I knew how), I received a message from Beverly Glenn, a DNA close family to first cousin match, It simply read, "We are a match, can we talk?"

I did not get back to her immediately (was it because I was busy or apprehensive, I cannot say). About a month later, I went on Ancestry.com to reply. There was another message from Beverly Glenn, and this one was more direct. It read, "I have been looking for a niece or nephew that would be in their mid-50s born in San Bernardino County. I have been searching for over forty years for them." I was stunned to realize *that's me*. I was so excited I was speechless. My husband typed my reply as my hands were shaking. Beverly and I agreed to talk the next night. I could only think about what I would learn and asked myself why an aunt was searching for me.

When I first called Aunt Beverly, I was extremely excited and extremely nervous. I did not know what to say, and I had not planned anything either. I learned that Aunt Beverly was my biological father's younger sister. She looked up to him, and they were remarkably close. Both of my biological parents (Paul and Linda) were deceased. Wow! I laid awake the whole night, deeply saddened and holding my dog. I just could not sleep.

Paul grew up in the Barstow/Hinkley area and died at age twenty-nine from cancer (probably from the water poisoning made famous in the *Erin Brockovich* movie). Aunt Beverly told me all about Paul and e-mailed me some pictures. To my surprise, my son Josh strongly resembles him. I learned I was not a secret; the family hoped I was okay and wanted to meet me.

The first week, Aunt Beverly and I talked every night, and every morning I woke up to a beautiful e-mail from her, each one perfectly worded. For the first time in my life, I had information, and I had a family medical history. Aunt Beverly sent me some of Paul's personal items: his driver's license, ID cards, and the only picture Aunt Beverly had of Linda. Linda had inscribed the picture with a note to Paul on the back. Paul carried it in his wallet. It read, "Paul, I haven't known you long, and already I'm crazy about you! Please don't ever leave me!".

Aunt Beverly started her search for me forty years ago by filling out a "Consent for Contact" form with the adoption agency. My parents were contacted and declined the request. I was a teen at the time. I understand their decision. However, if my parents were not going to tell me then, I wish they had at least told me when I was older. It would have been too late to meet Paul, but maybe I could have met Linda and other relatives and tell them I had a loving family and a good life.

Aunt Beverly made a family album for me and included

many pictures, stories, and genealogical information. Her package weighed eighteen pounds. Shortly after talking with Aunt Beverly, I spoke with Uncle David, Paul's younger brother. He shared more stories about Paul and the family. His mother had written the prayer focus for her church for many years. He had collected them and bound them in a book. David sent me a copy, and in the back of the book, he had made an update to include me in the listing as a grandchild. I was beginning to feel very connected to the Glenn family.

I put scrapbooks together for Aunt Beverly and Uncle David. It enabled me to look at my life as I collected pictures and stories to share. I was reminded how fortunate I have been in my life.

Linda died when she was fifty-nine. Before that, she would visit the Glenn family and talk about me. Aunt Beverly and Uncle David shared as much information with me as they could about her. However, I did not know her cause of death. I needed her death certificate to learn more. To obtain her death certificate, I needed to know her mother's maiden name. It took me thirty days of researching on Ancestry.com to figure out Linda's family tree. I do not know what made it more complicated, the fact that I was a rookie researcher or that my second great grandfather was Mormon, had three wives and twenty-two children, and two of his wives were sisters! With the help of DNA matches that shared their family trees, I was able to figure out the information I needed. *Hooray!* Upon receiving death certificates for Linda and her parents, I learned she had died from heart disease, as did her father. Wow, big reality check; I now monitor my cholesterol closer and have significantly improved my numbers. This may add years to my life.

I had received so much; however, I hoped for more. I wanted to know more about Linda. Unbeknownst to me, Aunt Beverly had mailed letters to every known address where Linda had lived. One person responded, a previous landlord, and we spoke on the phone. She said Linda talked about me extensively. I was not a secret. She also became reclusive and depressed around the holidays. It was not her choice to give me up for adoption. Linda was only seventeen when I was born. Therefore, I was in the custody of her mother. According to the landlord, Linda's mother chose to put me up for adoption. The landlord said Linda *hated* her mother for that decision. According to Aunt Beverly and Uncle David, they appear to have made peace later in life. I hope so. As it happened, Linda and her mother died less than two weeks apart.

Neither Paul nor Linda had other children. Linda herself was an only child. This makes Aunt Beverly and Uncle David, my closest living biological relatives.

In November 2018, I flew to California to meet Aunt Beverly. I went alone; my husband was unable to go with me. The plan was to spend the weekend at her home. I was nervous, but I felt like I already knew her since we talked on the phone every Monday night for the past three months. I was excited; we were finally meeting. I was coming down the escalator at the airport when I first saw her. She did not see me yet. She was holding a big sign with my name on it and a large bouquet of roses. Her daughter Amy, my cousin, was there with her husband, Keith. Aunt Beverly hugged me and held me. It was a beautiful union. It was such a special time; we were happy just to be together. We celebrated. I was amazingly comfortable with Aunt Beverly. Aunt Beverly wears a special necklace. It contains a diamond that Paul had bought years ago. She wanted me to have something special and presented me with a beautiful double heart necklace with two small sapphires on it to represent Paul and Linda. I felt special.

In April 2019, I met Uncle David. My husband and I stayed with him for a night. I was emotional and could sense that Uncle David was too. We shared stories. I wish the visit could have been longer. We looked at family pictures, and Uncle David presented me with a DVD with videos from two family reunions. It was amazing to see and hear the family. Especially my grandfather's voice. David gave me a tool chip that my grandfather had used at work. A tool chip is a small round disk with a number on it that my grandfather used to identify himself at the railroad company and check out specialized tools. He worked on train engines. Uncle David also gave me Paul's high school yearbooks so I could read the comments and know just how special everyone thought he was.

My aunt also wrote to Linda's cousin's wife. The cousin, Jack, handled Linda's parents' estate and had since died. His wife, Modena, reached out to me with a letter that started with, "So happy to know we have more family to love."

Modena had not known about me. In fact, of Modena's three children, her two oldest were adopted. She sent me five pictures of Linda, one of which my husband thought was me. Like my biological mother and her father, Jack also died from heart disease. Just when I thought this could not get any better, it did. In May 2019, my husband and I traveled to Arkansas and met Modena. She made us lunch, and we talked and shared stories. Modena presented me with a huge surprise. She had a pocket watch that belonged to my grandmother's father and a railroad watch that had been my grandfather's. He was a conductor. Modena and her three children wanted me to have those items and gifted them to me.

My brother recently asked me how my *other* family was. I thought for a moment and replied I do not have another family; I have a bigger family. My biological family has lovingly drawn me into the fold as if they had been waiting for me to show up. It saddens me that Paul and Linda died so young and that I will never meet them, although family and friends have given me a wonderful sense of who they were. My parents know that I have connected with my biological family and are happy for me. My mom and Aunt Beverly have met and continue to correspond.

My connection to my biological family completes my story and makes me feel closer to myself and my parents as I appreciate them even more. When I look in the mirror, I know who I look like and feel happy. All these people have shaped who I am, either by nature or nurture. My biological grandparents were all prayerful people. From before I was born, they prayed for me, and God answers prayers.

Sally's Story, Adoptive Mom

I welcome this opportunity to share with you the story of how I came to be Robyn's mother.

After my husband and I (Bob and Sally) had been married several years and were unsuccessful in starting a family of our own, we began thinking about adoption. Finally, in 1963 we decided to begin the process. We made an appointment with the adoption agency and met with the social worker assigned to us. We told her we were very much ready to adopt a little girl or little boy. After a series of nerve-wracking interviews at her office and visits to our home, we were approved.

What an exciting time for us! We began to prepare the nursery, carefully selecting the paint color and buying a crib and all of the things we would need to welcome our baby to its forever home. We painted the room a soft yellow, with white furniture. It was so cheery. After anxious months, we finally heard from our social worker. I was at work when I received a call from her that they had a baby girl for us. I remember shrieking with joy (no doubt startling my boss, a dentist, and his patients) and called my husband with the happy news. He rushed home, and we put the finishing touches on the nursery.

The next day we drove to the adoption agency, extremely excited and more than a little nervous. Our lives

were about to change! The social worker told us about
our new daughter: she was born two months premature on
December 25, 1963. She weighed only four pounds-thirteen
ounces and had been in foster care under a pediatrician's
supervision. When we adopted her on March 26, 1964, she
weighed eight pounds and four ounces. The social worker
brought her in and gently placed her in my arms. Here she
was, at last, a precious and adorable bundle of joy. Our
hearts melted.

The social worker left us alone for a while so we could
forever cherish this special moment with Robyn. Her eyes
were a beautiful blue; she had dimples, little or no hair, and
a cute little rosebud mouth. She looked perfect to Bob and
me. The foster family had named her Sunny, which was a
good name for her, but my husband and I had already decided on her name. We chose Robyn Rae in honor of my
mom and Robyn's grandmother. It seemed to suit her.

We left the agency, and I held my baby all the way
home, gazing at her. We couldn't believe our good for-
tune. We have our baby — and the beginning of a new chapter for all three of us. When we arrived home, Robyn was
a little fussy and tired, so I warmed up some formula and
held her while she took it. She fell asleep in my arms, looking so adorable. That first night we kept looking in on her
to make sure all was well. She had colic for a month or so,
which was very worrisome to us. After all, we didn't know
anything about being parents, but over the days and weeks,
it all became so natural to us. For me, a favorite moment
was holding Robyn while I gave her a bottle. She would

gaze up at me while holding one of my fingers. I treasured those times.

Robyn's grandparents, Grandmother and Papa, were so excited to meet her that they came over the very next day after her arrival. They were thrilled to hold their first grand-daughter. In the days following, there was a steady stream of relatives and friends to meet the new addition to our family. Robyn was welcomed and loved by all.

Robyn's Dad and I delighted in her early milestones: sitting, crawling, and her first words ("mama," "dada," and "bye-bye"). We played pat-a-cake and peek-a-boo, which made her giggle. At fourteen months, she took her first steps and started getting some hair, a pretty light brown.

We celebrated her first birthday on Christmas Day, 1964. Our Christmas baby! Her grandparents came over for dinner and birthday cake. And of course, she received lots of nice presents. Grandmother and Papa gave her a pretty blue coat and hat that matched her eyes. Robyn got her first baby doll and named her Phyllis. (Later, when her hair started looking unruly, she changed her name to Phyllis Diller.) She became her favorite doll. Robyn's Aunt Margaret and Uncle Oscar gave her a doll cradle for rocking Phyllis and Mrs. Beasley (another favorite) and many other dolls and stuffed animals. Robyn liked to play *house*, dressing up in my high heels, and putting on some lipstick. We would sometimes have tea parties, and she would set out her little tea set at her little table for her dolls and me. She liked having stories read to her and became a good reader.

Storytime was always at bedtime, with a little snuggling before turning out the lights.

We had family birthday parties for Robyn's first two years. For her third birthday, we invited her playmates and their moms for a sit-down lunch. Her favorite dish at the time was a tuna casserole which she wanted me to make for her friends. She was such a good little hostess. For her later birthday parties, it was usually cake and ice cream. For games, we had a pinata at some of her parties, and at other times instead of "pin the tail on the donkey," we played "pin the star on the Christmas tree." Since she was a Christmas baby, we thought that was a good idea. Those are such wonderful memories. As Robyn got older, we started celebrating her birthdays on March 26, the date we adopted her. Celebrating her adoption day was especially important to us and has been for fifty-seven years.

Robyn was about four-and-a-half when we decided the time was right to complete our family and adopt a baby boy. When the three of us arrived at the adoption agency, the social worker wanted Robyn to feel an important part of this special occasion, so she was the first to meet her baby brother. We named him Michael Robert, yet another Robert. We called him Mike. She was such a sweet big sister to him.

During her growing up years, we worried about her health, about the allergies she had developed, and the bouts of asthma that were sometimes severe. My heart went out to her during those difficult times. It was so hard seeing Robyn so sick. I would have changed places with her if I could.

We took Robyn on many outings to Knott's Berry Farm, Griffith Park Zoo, Disneyland, lots of fun places. She enjoyed being with her grandparents, and they so loved her, as did all her relatives. Her grandmother and Papa took us all out on their cabin cruiser for an exciting voyage around Newport Bay. She was a cute little sailor! Her aunt Margaret and uncle Oscar gave Robyn her first tricycle and a little rocking chair just her size.

Then it was time for Robyn to go to kindergarten. I cutely fixed her hair and bought her a darling new plaid dress. She looked so cute. We took pictures, and then we walked to the school just a few blocks away. Her playmates, Jody and Stacy, were in the same class. I could hardly wait until she got out of school. I met her, and we walked home together. She told me all about her teacher and what she had learned. It was a good first day.

Along with grade school, Robyn took ballet classes and looked so cute in her tutu. She took piano lessons from a lady in our neighborhood. Like me, she didn't like to practice, so that didn't last long. She joined Brownies and went on to Girl Scouts and earned many badges. I was her troop's Girl Scout Cookie chairman. My goodness, our living room was stacked high with cartons of cookies. We sold lots of cookies!

In high school, she wanted to take horseback riding lessons. So, we enrolled her in a riding academy, and she took hunter-jumper lessons. Watching her jumping hurdles made me nervous at first, but she always stayed in the saddle. (That is where she met Gary, another hunter-jumper student.) She continued with lessons, and before long, she wanted her very own horse. So, with money she had saved from her job as a hostess at a local restaurant, she bought a quarter horse and named him Tom. He was such a gentle horse and would follow her around the stable like a pet. Then Robyn became interested in dressage, sold Tom, and bought Camille, a thoroughbred that she trained for this demanding discipline. She took great care of her horses, as she did all of her pets, including her cat Christmas that she got for Christmas when she was in grade school.

Watching Robyn grow up was a joy, even when she was curious about her adoption. I recall that on Christmas Day, when she was ten years old, while waiting for her grandparents to come over for dinner, she asked me if I thought that her natural mother ever thought about her on this day. That brought tears to my eyes. I reassured her that, of course, she did and would always wonder about her. I know that she was curious about her birth parents through the years, and I understood that. From the very beginning, when she was old enough to understand, we read her a storybook about adoption. We always wanted her to know about being adopted, and we told her what little we knew about her birth parents. We wanted to be completely open with her. Just as we wanted her to know how we chose her to be ours and how incredibly special she was to us.

Then came graduation from high school, then a year in junior college, then a job. Where did the time go?

In the meantime, Gary graduated from college, and the two of them got back together. I remember when she became engaged and was so excited. As were we! Everyone was thrilled for her, but I especially remember when Robyn and Gary shared the news with Grandmother and Papa. They were so happy for her!

It was fun planning a wedding with Robyn and picking out her gown. She was a beautiful bride, and her dad and I were so happy for her and Gary. Three years later, she had a darling baby boy that they named Josh.

I am so proud of Robyn and the woman she has become, a wonderful, sweet, sensitive, and loving wife and mother. I am so blessed to be her mother.

And now Robyn has connected with some of her natural relatives. What an adventure this has been for her! Although the revelation was very emotional for me at first, I deeply appreciate her sharing the unfolding story of her birth parents and for introducing me to her aunt Beverly. Our bond was immediate, never an awkward moment, and we look forward to more times together. I know how much all this means to my daughter and to me as well.

In Robyn's senior year in high school, our social worker informed us that Robyn's unnamed biological aunt (Beverly) had filed a request to contact her. My husband and I denied the request, feeling strongly that so much was going on in Robyn's teenage life that the timing wasn't in her best interest. In hindsight, I regret not sharing this with Robyn as she got older.

It has been the greatest of joys to be Robyn's mother and watch her grow from a darling baby to womanhood. She is a kind, caring, and loving daughter. Bob and I are so immensely proud of her. The fact is, adopting her and Mike was the best and most rewarding decision we ever made.

What fun to recall and share these recollections of my daughter's early years. The story of Robyn's journey is a gift to her and all her family.

Beverly's Story, Birth Aunt

What? My brother Paul had a child? I was at my mom's, standing in her living room next to her, sitting in her favorite lime green chair, as she shared this info.

I was shocked!

It was 1975. Paul had been dead for three years. Shockingly and unexpectedly and suddenly, he died at age twenty-nine from cancer in 1971.

Mom said the child was a girl, and she was born on Christmas Day. I was shocked. I was just so shocked. I had never heard this information before.

As far back as I can remember, I was remarkably close to my brother Paul. I've even been called Paul's shadow. He was eight years older than me. He was level-headed, mechanically inclined, kind, handsome, popular, a football player, a good dancer, and a nice dresser. He liked gas-powered model airplanes, shooting guns, and old cars. We lived on twenty-six-aces of sagebrush, five and a half miles from PG&E (Pacific Gas and Electric), in Hinkley, outside Barstow, California.

He was always nice to me, always coming to the rescue of the bickering between my three-year older brother and me. In all reality, Paul probably took pity on me being the youngest—but he was my hero.

In high school, Paul had a job at Idle Spurs—the fanciest restaurant in town. I didn't know at the time that he was a busboy; for all I knew, he was next in line to be the owner. The place was too expensive for our family to go there for dinner.

I grew up watching *Dick Clark* and *Soul Train*, two music and dance shows. I could dance pretty well, too. Paul said he wished he could take me to the local club that had dance contests. He knew we'd win, but I was too young.

After I heard the news of Paul's child, I wondered and wondered and wondered, *Is she okay? Does she need anything?* I felt this responsibility to Paul to help, do what I could, but I didn't know how or what to do.

I started by writing to the San Bernardino adoption agency. I was shocked and more than a little surprised when my letter landed on the desk of the lady who handled the original adoption in 1963. She wrote back kindly and perplexed, skeptical, wondering why it was the aunt who was writing and not one of the biological parents. I wrote again explaining Paul had died in 1971, and I enclosed Paul's death certificate.

The adoption lady was always kind in her letters, explaining it was a closed adoption and no information could be released, but not to give up. One of her letters included a form I could fill out to have on file in case the child ever came looking for information. With this form on file, my contact information would be provided to her so we could be connected.

On and on through the years, I wondered if the child was okay or if she needed anything. At least, I wanted her to know how special Paul is, in my opinion. And I wanted her to know that our family is a good family, hardworking, middle-class people. She would be proud of us. I believed that Paul would be disappointed in us if we didn't try to reach her.

Time went on. I saved those inquiring letters I wrote to the San Bernardino adoption agency—it was three-plus decades of writing. I had assembled a photo album with photographs of our Glenn family. I mailed it to the adoption agency worker; she wrote saying it would be saved for her in her file. Then when my first grandchild arrived in 1993, I sent photographs of him too to be placed in her file if she ever contacted the adoption agency in the future for biological information.

From time to time, Linda Meadows, her biological mother, would stop by our family home. We'd catch up with what was going on in everyone's lives. And we would talk about this baby girl out there, somewhere. Linda talked about trying to find this child. I shared with her that I've been writing letters to the adoption agency for information but no contact yet.

I remember Linda very well. To me, she was tall and beautiful, blondish hair, big smile—always smiling, graceful, kind, upbeat, pleasant demeanor, polished, relaxed, elegant—a person would feel comfortable from the start when being with her. Paul always had the nicest girlfriends, and some stayed in touch over the years.

In 2002 my mom passed away unexpectedly. I was hoping the child would get to meet my mom; we called her grandma GG (a.k.a great-grandma), but that meeting had not happened. I was beginning to believe many defeating beliefs, such as she didn't know she was adopted, or she didn't want to know us. I put my letters in my important files and told my daughter to continue the search if I die before meeting her. I hadn't given up, but the hope of contact was fading. Maybe Amy would meet her someday.

My daughter, Amy, and I talked about my brother Paul and his daughter over the years. I didn't want him to disappear into our family history. He was alive in my thoughts, photos of him in my mom's home, in our family conversations, in my stories, things I learned from him—he was alive just in a different way.

I came across a distant cousin in 2017, Carol Andrews, in Carthage, Missouri. We talked and talked about the Glenn family history; she knew about many generations back that I didn't know about. She encouraged me to do a

DNA test to verify where we were related. I did the test in 2018. In looking at the DNA results, the information was all foreign to me.

My good friend Wynn, a genealogy expert, had found an eighty-six-year-old brother who didn't know anything about her. My other friend Nancy, her husband, had been adopted, and they found his biological family when he was in his 70s. They encouraged me not to give up looking for this baby girl.

When I received my Ancestry.com DNA results, my friend Wynn stopped by to decipher for me what I was looking at on the Ancestry.com DNA test results. When Wynn saw the high percentage of relationship connection to the first name on the list, she said, "This could be our baby girl." Unsure and in disbelief, we both looked at each other with eyes wide open, jaw-dropping mouths, and gasped.

Wynn pulled out a relationship chart and convinced me this could be the baby girl—I was over the moon. Then I became afraid I might scare her off unexpectedly by not using the right words when emailing. Wynn said, "Tell her everything." I was reluctant to email everything; I didn't want to scare her away. *First impressions are hard to change*, I thought. I emailed her a vague message—no response. I was out of town, and Wynn checked on me several times, asking, "Did you hear from her?" "No, not yet," was my reply. "Send her a second message," Wynn commanded. I did. I sent another fluffy, wordy message. Finally, I got a reply. Yay! This time I wrote more information, including that I had been looking for her for forty years.

I learned her name is Robyn.

We emailed daily back and forth for a week or two. Questions after questions. The first questions Robyn had were, "What are my biological parents' names, and what's their medical history?" My heart was so heavy when telling her Paul had passed on. Oh, she was sad. I shared my thought that we could provide enough information about Paul and Linda to give her a good sense of them.

We emailed a date and time to talk on the telephone. July 16, 2018. The phone rang; we introduced ourselves. After that, there was a long, long pause—I just didn't know what to say; there was so much to share. And so much I wanted to learn. We began to talk, and she asked if we had ever thought about her. It was hard to explain the magnitude that I'd been looking for her for forty years.

We emailed photos back and forth. *Wow*, I thought, *she's beautiful*. She has Linda's beautiful smile and Paul's thick dark hair and beautiful skin. (Upon meeting her, she has Linda's beautiful, elegant demeanor too.)

In my quest to know what to say and what not to say, I looked online for an adoption counseling group in Sacramento. In speaking to the counselor on the phone, she said, "I can tell you're very excited to find her and know you have a lot to share with her but slow down." That was particularly good advice. I stopped asking Robyn questions for a while to let her get all her questions answered first. I attended three different monthly group sessions. The attendees were happy to share with me what adoptees want to know; information and being accepted. I felt a little better knowing more about what to do and say. I made an angel crystal suncatcher for each one of those ladies to wish them well and love and peace.

I wanted Robyn to have photocopies of Paul and Linda and my family. I stood at Staples' copy machine, making copies for hours of family photos until I ran them out of photo paper. I stayed up late and got up early to type Robyn stories about Paul and our family. I wanted Robyn to know Paul, just like I'd mentally promised Paul—that she'd know about him and our family.

In our many emails and phone calls, I learned Robyn and Gary's 30th wedding anniversary was coming up. I was both astounded and amazed. *I have the perfect gift*, I thought. Years earlier, Paul had a great idea for our parents' 30th wedding anniversary. We went down to Tiny Time Jewelers and bought them a silver-plated pie stand. His idea to have it engraved "Happy 30th anniversary from Paul, Beverly, David."

After all these years, Mom had saved the pie stand, and after Mom and Dad's death, I saved it too—it was forty-seven years old. In thinking now, it seems that somehow Paul had bought that silver-plated pie stand for Robyn too—I think it was meant for her. I sent that 30th wedding anniversary silver-plated pie stand to Robyn and Gary for their 30th wedding anniversary. Mom and Dad's anniversary was in August, and Paul died in November.

I also learned that at one time, Robyn and her family lived about an hour from me, that she liked Boston terriers and attended dog shows, too. She even attended dog shows at our local fairgrounds; the turn-off is only one block from my home. So, for years we unknowingly took the same turnoff near my home.

Robyn and I set a date to meet in person, November 10, 2018—I could hardly wait. I'd pick her up at the airport. My daughter and son-in-law wanted to come too. We had fun making big signs to wave, so she'd spot us when coming down the airport escalators. I got a dozen roses to give to her too. We wanted her to know she was special, and we were happy to see her. We all had the biggest group hug ever.

On Robyn's first visit with me, I wanted to give her something nice and meaningful. In a local jewelry store, I saw a necklace with two hearts intertwined—to me, one heart represents Paul, and the other heart represents Linda. I asked the jeweler if he could insert a small sapphire inside each heart as both Paul and Linda's birthdays are in September. I was very pleasantly surprised when Robyn arrived wearing a sapphire ring—she shared it's one of her favorite stones.

Christmas was coming up. I usually send out a drug-store-made multi-photo Christmas card of my kids. Since I had connected with Robyn that summer, I included her photos on my drugstore multi-photo Christmas card. In my

Christmas narrative, I shared this is brother Paul's daughter. Cousins wrote back saying, "It's about time" and "It's great to know her." One of the points I learned from the adoption counseling group was they wanted to be accepted. The multi-photo Christmas card with several photos of Robyn and her family on it went over great— the family welcomed her all aboard. It was sort of like a delayed baby announcement but on a Christmas card.

My grandmother, Anna Hetrick, made a blanket for all the grandkids and great-grandkids. The top was patchwork; the backside is flannel. I have one; Amy has one too. I noticed many years back in my hope chest that I have two. Seems like Grandmother Anna made a blanket for Robyn years before, and I had it just waiting for Robyn to show up.

The next summer, Robyn got to visit me again and brought Gary this time. On this trip, Robyn first visited her mom, then they all drove halfway to my home so they could stay with me a bit. I met Robyn's mom for the first time. I was a little nervous but more excited and vastly wanted to meet her mom, Sally. I instantly felt welcomed and comfortable. It was fantastic to finally meet her, this wonderful woman who opened her heart for Robyn since birth, keeping her safe and well-loved. Sally is the beacon in Robyn's life that somehow fate knew Robyn needed.

Now I can stop wondering if Robyn's okay or if she needs anything. She's more than okay; she had a wonderful childhood and has a wonderful family. I'm happy. I accomplished my promise to my brother Paul—Robyn knows all about him.

1. Linda, Robyn's birth mom
2. Paul, Robyn's birth dad
3. Bob, Sally and Robyn on her brother Michael's adoption day
4. Robyn and Aunt Beverly meeting for the first time

Devon

Tari (Devon's mom) and I have known each other for probably fifteen years, on and off. We met working out together at jazzercise most days. I recall her bringing her children to babysitting during class. I knew they were adopted but never asked questions. Fast-forward to last year (2020), when this project was birthed by my own experience, I thought of her family. When I reached out to Tari, she was happy to share their story with us. I have followed her children growing mainly on social media these days. I am excited to include this family's story of international adoption.

Devon's Story

Because I've known I am adopted my whole life, I really don't give it much thought. It wasn't a mystery to me; it wasn't something that was hidden from me. I have a picture of her, my birth mom, Victoria, holding me. That's helpful. We can tell little things like we have the exact same shape fingers; our facial structure is exactly the same; our eyes are exactly the same. I know where I came from, so that is a comfort, but there was never really a point where I remember asking too many questions. I never noticed the whole race thing. I've always seen both of them as my parents; there was no question in my mind about that.

Tari's Story, Adoptive Mom

I was six years old the very first time I remember thinking about adoption. I went into the doctor's office for my annual physical, and he put his stethoscope on my stomach and, joking around, said, "I can already hear a baby kicking around in there." I was horrified. I remember at six years old thinking, *That's not right because I'm going to adopt my babies. He's got to be wrong.* I thought about adoption often over my lifetime because I found out about my heart condition when I was sixteen.

Before my husband Jim and I ever decided to start a family, we thought long and hard about whether we wanted to have a biological child because of my heart condition. Although we felt overwhelmed at the thought of adoption, my heart was led to adoption. We decided to try to have a biological child, and I put an extremely strict time limit on it. We tried for eight months to get pregnant, and the whole time (from day one), I researched adoption. That's where we ended up going because we didn't get pregnant in those eight months.

We initially investigated domestic adoption. At the time, my heart condition was a roadblock to domestic adoption because biological mothers want a healthy adoptive mom. And while I knew that I would need surgery in the future, I believed that I would make my way through.

I wouldn't choose someone with a health condition if I were a biological mother either, so domestic adoption did not seem to be the choice for us. We also worried about losing our child if a biological parent came back. Now on the back end of that, I have a vastly different perspective because I would give anything to be able to introduce my kids to their birth parents. Having watched them grow up, I'm so proud of them, and I desperately desire for their birth parents to receive the gift of knowing what they gave the world.

My medical concerns and our fear that we would never get a baby led us to international adoption. In our home studies for international adoption, we were able to go into less depth about my medical issues. I received a letter from my cardiologist saying that my condition wouldn't affect my longevity, and through international adoption, that was sufficient.

We originally researched adoption from Russia because we had concerns about having a child that didn't look like us and dealing with the social ramifications of that. Unfortunately, there were a lot of things that concerned us about Russian adoption. First, I had no desire to go to Russia, and we would have been required to make that trip. Second, it seemed to be a very shady adoption system, which made us feel uncomfortable. And we also worried about the potential for our child to have oppositional defiant disorder (ODD). I learned that many kids from Russia come home with fetal alcohol syndrome. This was when I started researching countries where babies tend to be healthier, and Guatemala was the first one that came up. Soon after, we attended an international family function to meet other adoptive families and just ask them questions.

At this event, we ran into a woman who brought home a healthy three-month-old baby from Guatemala. Although I had researched Russian adoption for eight months, we switched countries and sent off our first paperwork for Guatemala two weeks later. Seven months later, Devon came home to us; it was extremely fast.

Most referrals people received were for newborn babies. Devon was already seven weeks old, so we know Victoria (his birth mother) tried to keep him. Because we wanted to experience as much of the "baby phase" as possible, knowing he would already be seven weeks older at homecoming and not knowing how long the adoption process would take, we felt uncertain about accepting his referral. We're beyond grateful we chose not to worry about that!

When we received Devon's referral and saw his pictures, he was wearing a little onesies baseball uniform. Jim is a baseball player; he played in college. When Jim said, "That's our sign, it's him," I agreed, and we accepted his referral. We got his paperwork in the mail a few days later. Before I opened it, I said a little prayer, "If the birth mom's birthday is either mine or Jim's, I know this baby was meant to be ours," then I opened the envelope. I saw that his birth mom's birthday was in December, and I was thinking, "Oh my God, oh my God, oh my God." I shifted the paper over so I could see the day, and it was my birthday, December 13 (we are exactly ten years apart in age). It was incredible, and at that point, there was no question in my mind. I said a prayer, and God answered. It felt like He was screaming in my ear, "Yes, this is your baby." God made it as clear to me as He possibly could. It was an astonishing moment I'll never forget.

We got to visit Dev in Guatemala before his adoption was finalized. We lived together in a hotel room in Antigua for a week, and then I had to give him back. I went home without him, and it very nearly killed me. I sank into a depression and could barely get out of bed. I was terrified to go alone but ended up flying back a month later by myself on September 8, 2001. I rented a room in a house with some other adoptive moms. This was the moment we were reunited. Three days later, 9/11 happened. I was right where I was meant to be. I would have surely lost my mind if I had been cut off from him at that fraught time. He was six months old. Jim was able to come down and be with us to finalize the adoption on September 20, and we headed home on the twenty-first.

From the day Devon came home at six months old, we told him his story. He was seven weeks old when his birth mom relinquished him because she wanted to keep him. And she just couldn't. She already had a three-year-old child. She was a single mom supporting her entire extended family, and she made $20 a month as a cook on a farm. When Devon was born, she lost her job. She got to the point where she realized she couldn't even feed this child.

When he was four months old, Victoria had to come back to the baby home, which was quite a journey from where she lived. Then she had to ride to Guatemala City with him, where they could have a DNA test to prove that he was hers so that he could be adoptable. If Victoria had not done that; if she had not come back and made that journey with him, he would not have been adoptable; he would have lived in this system until he was about fifteen, and then he would have been released on the streets. There were a lot of kids in the baby home who could never be adopted because their birth moms didn't come back for a DNA test. Victoria wanted him to have a family, so she made that heartbreaking journey. In the picture we have of them, he is sitting on her lap when they got their DNA test. She looks so sad in the picture. Just knowing she did that for him and how many kids did not have that benefit right there tells us what we need to know about her feelings for him.

For the first three years of his life, I sent stacks and stacks of pictures of him to the baby home in Guatemala. I wasn't allowed to have contact with his birth mom. If by chance she was able to find her way back to Guatemala City, she lived quite a distance away, and it was difficult for her to get there the first time; I wanted there to be pictures for her so she'd know he was okay. And so that she could see he was healthy, happy, and deeply loved.

I was concerned about the racial difference. I'm a white person, and everybody's like, "Oh, you must teach him about his culture." I felt like, yes, but I am not part of that culture, and I always worried about not being able to nurture that for him. But then I thought (and this is not an adoption-community-friendly opinion), his culture is he is a Latino being raised in a white family. This is a unique culture unto him, and that's not something that I can fix or replace, that's just his experience, so I stopped worrying about that.

People would say ugly stuff to me when my kids were little, and they thought the kids wouldn't understand. They would tell me that I should have adopted one of my own, that type of nastiness, or they would ask how much I paid for Skye, our adopted daughter from China. It was just horrible ugly stuff that made me truly angry. It was extremely hard for me to deal with those situations. Unfortunately, it happened a lot. As the kids got older and people knew that they would understand, they stopped asking those questions in front of them. Even today, we draw stares when we go out, especially when we're with Sindel, Dev's friend who is Black, and Skye and her friend who's Caucasian. Some people look at us like they are trying so hard to figure out our story, and they don't mean anything by it, but that gets annoying.

Devon went through a phase when he was three and four years old, where he did not believe that he didn't grow in my tummy. He did get really upset; he would say, "Yes, I did," and I'm explaining to him, "No, you didn't; you grew in Victoria's tummy." We went on like that for some time. It got so bad that I remember one time I was with my dad at a diamond broker, and Devon started talking about it, and I reminded him, "No, you didn't grow in my tummy," so he lifted my shirt and put his head on my stomach and said, "Yes, I did." It was hilarious!

I pushed both my kids to search for some sadness because I was always terrified that they would stuff their feelings or not talk to me about it. I always reassured them; it was okay to love their birth families. I wanted them to have thoughts of love for them, but if they were angry, that was okay too. And I encouraged them to talk to me about whatever they were thinking or feeling. I urged them to remember there's this woman in another country, and she's probably wondering where you are; if you're okay. Doesn't that make you sad? I wanted them to connect with that so badly so that they wouldn't grow up and then feel the sadness and have nowhere to go with it. They were really both just always okay with it. That was weird to me because I expected them to have some level of anger or sadness about the families that they didn't know. I imagined how I would feel in their shoes, and I would want those answers. Maybe my kids seem at ease with it because they've heard their stories since they were infants, so that's just their lives.

Devon is my emotional one; he's the one that feels things deeply. So, it worked out great that he is the one that we have the answers for. Maybe that is part of why he is so at peace. We had his adoption documents translated, so we know that she just couldn't take care of him. It's not that she didn't want him; she quite literally could not feed him. She wanted a better life for him, and he's had a wonderful life. I just wish she knew that; I wish she had the peace of knowing. I just think she'd be so crazy proud.

This woman signed her adoption documents with her thumbprint because she'd never gone to school; she didn't know how to read or write. Devon is going to nursing

school. I want Victoria to know that she did that; she gave
him that chance. Right now, it isn't a possibility, but I have
hope that someday somehow, we'll have a connection. I
wish Devon's birth mom could hear him play the guitar.
There are so many things about him that are so beautiful.
I want her to understand the gift she gave us. I want to be
able to express my gratitude to her. I probably want a connection to Victoria more than Devon.

I am a firm believer that our family was created the way
it was meant to be created. I feel like these kids were meant
to be my children. (That is also not a popular opinion in the
adoption community.) People get incredibly angry about
that sentiment and say things like, "Oh, you think your
child was meant to lose their birth culture; meant to lose
their birth family. You think God wanted that *nightmare* for
them?" My answer to them is an emphatic "No, of course
not. But God didn't want me to be raised by an abusive
father either, but that was a path of my life." People in the
adoption community can be very judgmental. We distanced
ourselves from the adoption community as the kids got older. Staying in touch with other adoptive parents with children from the same countries as ours was part of how we
were trying to pass down a little bit of their culture to them,
but it was kind of toxic. People have their opinions about
what was right and wrong in raising adopted children. We
just kind of rolled with what felt right to us, and I feel like
it worked out extremely well.

We feel incredibly blessed. We could not have dreamed
up better children for me. They're not perfect; nobody's

perfect, but they are the perfect puzzle pieces to my heart. I feel so blessed.

They are nineteen and sixteen now, and I still can't believe they're mine; I can't believe I get to be their mom. Still to this day, it trips me up, just how blessed I am.

Jim and Tari have been married for twenty-six years. They met in college, and Tari says she knew from their first date she'd be happy forever married to Jim. "My soul recognized his, and I knew we were meant to be together."

1. Tari and Devon meeting for the first time in Guatemala
2. Devon meeting his baby sister, Skye
3. Family photo; Tari, Sindel, Skye, Devon and Jim

Barb

I was introduced to Barb through her biological sister, Marissa, whom I have known for many years. I spoke with Barb over the phone, and she was open and willing to share her story with us. You'll see that Barb found a lot more than she was searching for when she connected with her family. I am grateful that she's allowed me to include her story here.

Barb's Story

When I was little, I always thought there were three ways of being born, natural, cesarean and adoption. I always knew I was adopted. The story in my head was of my parents going into a room full of babies and picking me out. It didn't quite happen that way, but I know they had adopted a son, and then three years later, they adopted me. We were both nine months old at adoption.

I wasn't on a search for my birth parents my entire life. I did get my original birth certificate when I was legally able. My curiosity was more about health issues and if there were really people who looked like me. I was also married and had children of my own, so naturally, I wanted health history. I wasn't so curious that I was willing to pay someone to find my birth mother. Internet searches brought up so many people with the same name as my birth mother. I always told people that I was adopted. I do remember one time we thought we *found* her and were going to drive by the house. We were wrong because my mom was married and had a different name by then. Good thing we didn't do it. Several friends wanted me to pursue finding my mom and were extremely excited for me when I connected with my birth family. As many things happen today, the entire event was recorded on Facebook.

My mom and dad, who raised me, loved me and supported me in everything I did. I had a good life. My mom and I did discuss what could happen if I found my birth mother. She made the point of what if she hadn't told anyone she gave me up, and I would ruin her life. I understood because it would be a pretty big secret to keep. Funny because that was one of the reasons my birth mother didn't try to find me, that maybe I didn't know I was adopted. My mom always told me to say a prayer for my birth mother on my birthday because she said she would probably be thinking about me that day. When I had my kids, I realized you always have a connection with them. Somehow when I prayed for her, I felt like she would know I was okay.

On March 18, 2015, I got a message on Facebook from someone who turned out to be my sister Johnna. Needless to say, it was quite a surprise. I had registered with an adoption registry that was there for people who wanted to find their children or parents. I figured that was one way of letting my birth mother know I was willing to meet. It's hard to believe that it's been six years already. It's also hard to believe that at sixty years old, I should meet my birth family.

We all agreed to meet at a restaurant, all but Marissa, who lives in Saint Louis, Missouri. Fortunately, our mom had told them about me, so it wasn't a total shock. Also, we had checked out each other's Facebook pages to find out as much as we could. My youngest sister, Melanie, was the most apprehensive about meeting me. Fortunately, everything went okay. There is definitely a family resemblance.

After spending more time with them, we have found similarities in our sense of humor. Also, one time when Melanie and I took a road trip to Marissa's, we were talking, and she stopped me and said how much I looked like our mom.

I have been blessed by how welcoming the whole family has been. I have met nieces, nephews, cousins, and other extended family. One time I was working at a concession stand at a baseball game, and someone came up to the stand and introduced themselves as a cousin. The oddest thing was that her younger son had been in a science class I taught. It's such a small world.

I grew up as the baby in my family. The transition to the oldest has been interesting. I often think about how different I would have been if I had grown up with my brother and sisters. I also think about what if I had met them at another point in my life.

I am sorry that I didn't get to meet my birth mother. I think if I had met her, I would have been able to tell her that she made the right decision. The family that I grew up in was loving and caring. My brother was also adopted so in a way that made things easier. We had an extended family that was quite close. One of the things that made me happy is knowing that she did think about me and told her other children about me. I was glad to hear the story of my birth and that the decision to give me up was not an easy one. I never thought it was, especially after having my own children.

Through Ancestry.com, I have also been able to begin connecting with my birth father's family. But that's a story for another day.

Marissa

I met Marissa many years ago, and we have stayed in touch through our church and, more recently, practicing yoga together. Marissa reached out to me about her family's story after reading a social media post last year (2020) about my personal adoption story. She shared with me about reuniting with her older sister.

Marissa's Story, Birth Sister: "My Mom's Baby"

Growing up, there were two things that my mom and I discussed that befuddled me. I am sure there were more, but these two stood out. I am the oldest in the family, but on my birth certificate, under the heading of live births, it reads one; as far as I knew, there were no other children older than me. When I discussed this with Mom, she just said it was a typo. The second thing was that sometime in April, every April, my mom would say, "You would be this many years old if I would have had you when I met your father." This I agreed with; it did not surprise me since it could be the anniversary of when they met; it was somewhere between my birthday of March 21 and my parent's anniversary of May 1. Her explanations of both things made perfect sense to me.

These two answers became all too clear to me when I was twenty years old. Mom told us that she had placed a little girl for adoption when she was nineteen. It was an *Aha* moment; there was one live birth before me. This news was a shock to me; I remember thinking, *I was not the oldest! How could this be?* Being so self-centered at twenty years old, I apparently said some things which caused my younger sisters to think that I would never want to meet this older sister, my mother's baby, whose name was Michelle. After thinking about this news for a while, I came to understand that I may not be the oldest of my mother's children, but I was still the oldest of my parents' union. Also, I already had two younger sisters who I am close to, sisters are nice to have, and I had another one. She proceeded to tell us that she had Michelle when she was living in an unwed mothers' home. Her mother (our grandmother) wanted to keep the baby but could not find anyone in the family to adopt her. Financially my mother could not take care of the baby, so after a few months, she placed her for adoption. Mom also told us that she met our dad right after she had given birth. Dad was aware of the baby since they had discussed going out to find her when they got married. My dad felt that Mom had placed her in a good home and for the right reasons. At that time, Michelle would have been five years old, and it would disrupt her whole life. That day was the only day in my memory that Mom talked about having a baby.

Years passed. My middle sister, then a social worker dealing with the adoptions of children, learned the rules for the state of Ohio in terms of adopted children and birth parents' finding each other. Over time she had considered talking to our mom about her baby but decided that she would not investigate. She was worried about how it would affect our dad, and due to my actions back when I was twenty, she was not sure how I felt about meeting this older sister. We had not talked about my feeling towards my mom's baby since that time when I was twenty. Fast forward many years, my mom died, and my younger sisters talked about finding my mom's baby. They discussed it with me, and I was all for it, having dealt with some of the issues.

After some discussion, they decided to talk to Mom's sisters, our aunts, about our mother's baby. My mother had two sisters, one sixteen months older and the other the baby of the family. My younger sisters met with both, and their stories were completely different from each other. Mom's older sister said she was twenty and had just gotten married when the baby was born. She also told us my grandmother approached them about adopting my mom's baby. My aunt felt that it was too soon in their marriage for a baby, so they told her no. Mom's younger sister remembered her father being so angry with my mother about being pregnant, he kicked mom out of the house, and my aunt was told not to talk about my mom ever again. My mother went to live with her aunt and uncle during this time, until just before giving birth, then lived in an unwed mothers' home. She placed her baby for adoption a few months after birth.

At this time, we stopped investigating and went no further. It was a few years later when, one afternoon, I received a call from a friend. She read that Ohio was opening its adoption records. She told me that when my mom died, she thought about how sad it was that my mom never got to see her baby again. With that thought in mind, and because it was a slow afternoon during my workday, I decided to search my mom on Google. I found my mom's obituary, nothing new there. I then changed the search parameters adding adoption. Google brought up the Adoption.com website, and there she was, Barbara LaPosh Mohner, a.k.a Michelle Marie Harmon, my mom's baby. All the facts listed on the site checked out. It was unbelievable that it was so easy. I immediately went to Facebook to check her out. She looked identical to me; she was definitely my sister. I was so excited. I immediately sent a text to my middle sister, "I found Mom's baby; check out Facebook." She called me after checking Facebook. We were both ecstatic, nervously ecstatic. What should be our next steps? First, we sent a text to our other two siblings. Then we decided to have a family conference with the original four of us; we were nervous. If we reached out, would she want to keep in contact with us? We felt vested in her; we had known about her, she had not known about us, but it was her story. In our family, sister is not just a word; it means something more than just a passing face.

We decided our first step was to direct message her on Facebook, to tell her about us, four siblings that she did not know she had, and that sadly Mom had passed away. Then the wait, with nervousness, did she get on Facebook? Would she want anything to do with us? We are a loud, boisterous family with a weird sense of humor; would we scare her away? We patiently waited for her response, which was not long, like the very next morning. There was relief that she wanted to talk to all of us and meet us. From that message, our relationship moved forward; a few days later, we had our first phone conversation. Two weeks later, the four siblings living in Cleveland met for the first time. From afar, I told them to be nice to her, not to scare her away because I wanted to get the chance to meet her. They all called after dinner; their stories were all the same. They felt that they had been together forever. The next day Mike, Barb's husband, posted a feel-good Monday Facebook story. It read, "As many of you know, my wife is adopted, and last night, she got to meet three of the four siblings that she did not know about until a few weeks ago. We felt like we had known them all her life, and yes, Marissa, they did not scare her away". I was able to meet her a few weeks after that.

At first, our relationship began as a get-to-know each other discussion with a person that looked a lot like me, a sister, but whom I knew nothing about. I was cautious with what I said because I did not want to lose her after I had just found her. Her birthday is April 15, which was the second puzzle piece, the date when my mom would tell me I would be this many years old, right between my birthday and my parents' anniversary. I was able to tell her that our mom had thought about her, and she wanted the best for her. My mom met my dad right after she gave birth to Barb, but it was Barb's birthday when my mom mentioned this to me. We share many similarities; she has some talents of my mom. My mom was an avid seamstress, so is Barb. She has a daughter named Melissa, who is a mechanical engineer; I am an electrical engineer. Her son Mickey has the same red hair as me, is an accountant like my other nephew, and they share the same birthday. All five of us have the same sense of humor.

It has been five years since that day, and our relationship feels like we have always been together. We went from her being my mom's baby to my older sister. Over the last five years, we have shared a lot of good times and now have some shared memories; it is hard to remember a time when she was not there. I am glad that we were not afraid to take the leap, and we reached out to find her.

1. Barb with her mom and brother, Greg
2. Patricia, Barb's birth mom
3. Barb and her birth siblings

Dede

I met Dede at yoga practice. She was an instructor along with Robyn, whom you've already met. At the time, about twelve years ago now (maybe more), I had never practiced yoga, and this was a fun Saturday morning event with some girlfriends. After practice, we were talking, and she invited me to attend her church. I found out later she was the pastor's wife at that church. I knew the church because it was just down the street from my home. You'll read more of my faith journey in my story. Soon after, I began regularly attending yoga practice with Dede, and over time, we became friends. We've grown much closer over the past four years, and she shared her adoption story with me. We talked many times about my story, too, which I did not share often. I craved her perspective. She was one of the first people I reached out to with the news of my reunion. She has supported me in so many ways through my journey this past year. I am profoundly grateful for her friendship and her willingness to freely share her story and insights with us.

Dede's Story: "Quite Anxious"

I am the daughter of Kathy and Tom's love affair.

Two spirited teens arrived at Eastern Kentucky University (EKU) to realize they had been childhood acquaintances who saw each other at annual horse shows. For as long as they could remember, they'd had a crush on one another.

Each had experienced family traumas and felt an exhilarating freedom to finally be away at college.

My mother and father were attractive, ambitious, and possessed magnetic personalities. Kathy had pretty blonde-brown hair, a beautiful smile, almond-shaped eyes, and elegant hands. She was passionate about education and exceptional in math. Tom was tall, dark, and handsome; some say he resembled Clark Gable. He had always loved school, having developed a strong work ethic, excelling in English, enjoying intramural sports, and developing a keen interest in studying psychology.

They loved to go dancing together.

One night at a party, I was conceived. An unwanted pregnancy at the onset of bright, new possibilities. A back-and-forth struggle ensued; their mothers finally got involved and made the decision about what would be best for my future and well-being.

The year was 1966, a time when no emotional resources were available for unwed teenage mothers. Shockingly, these vulnerable teen moms *disappeared* or *went away* for a while. Later they quietly reappeared, with an internalized message of "we won't talk about this again." Even now, and especially around Mother's Day, I still can't fully comprehend the emotional trauma these fragile young women endured.

That's exactly what Kathy did. She went away to live with her aunt and uncle at their lake home for the duration of the pregnancy. Tom continued his undergrad education at EKU.

I was born on October 5, and Kathy gave me the name Alicia. She was able to hold me for less than two hours, then handed me over to a kind social worker named Kitty. Kathy's mother, Nan, was there. Kathy and Nan requested that Kitty let them know I had been adopted into a good home. Kitty assured them she would.

I was fostered by a presbyterian minister and his wife for two months, then adopted by Bob and Betty in December as their first child. They named me Deandra (a hybrid of their fathers' names, Dee and Andrew), with the nickname "Dede." I had weighed a little over six pounds at birth and was still petite when they held me for the first time. They dressed me in a pretty pink outfit and took me to our new home.

Kathy continued her education by way of a significant detour. Tom graduated from EKU, joined the Marines, and eventually went to law school. The two never reconnected or re-kindled their love affair. Rather, each moved on to eventually find new loves and establish their respective lives.

My earliest recollection of my adoption is age five. My parents had read the recommended books at the time and sought to use sensitive, encouraging language about my adoption. I heard words like *chosen* and *special*. Among

the most tender and meaningful of all my experiences was
Mom coming into my room every October 5. She would
sit with me on my bed, put her arm around me, and say,
"I know she's thinking about you today." And I always,
always believed that Kathy *was* thinking about me. As I
became older, Mom added, "If you ever want to search for
your birth mother, I will help you. If I were you, I would
want to know." Mom went even further to gently stress that
I would need to be certain I was emotionally prepared to
receive an answer of yes or no, "Because they may already
have a family of their own, and the others may not know
about you."

*How reasonably delicate for every person involved in
this process.*

Almost all adoptions in 1966 were closed ones. The records were sealed. The process of searching for one's birth
parents began by petitioning the court. Only the adoptee
had search privileges. The birth parent (almost always the
birth mother) would be contacted. She had the right to remain open to being contacted or to respectfully refuse the
contact. If she were open, she would offer her contact information and wait. It would then become the adoptee's choice
to pursue the contact. If the birth mother refused contact,
the search ended there.

I grew up in a conservative Christian home. We were
Baptists who lived in Western Kentucky. Dad was a dentist;
Mom, a radiology technician by vocation, chose to become
a homemaker and full-time mother. Mom couldn't get preg-

nant. She told me she'd slipped out of church every Mother's Day, went to the car, and cried tears of sadness and shame. Two years after bringing me "home," as they would say, Mom and Dad adopted another child, my brother Kevin. He was two weeks old, "The son of a military officer, who had a reputation of being a playboy."

The elusive stories.

Two years later, Mom became pregnant, a miracle baby named Karen. Sweet, and the spitting image of both Mom and Dad. We loved her so. I can honestly say my parents never treated any of us with favoritism. We were three distinctly different personalities with entirely different needs.

I was given every opportunity: piano lessons, swim team, academic school trips, cheerleading, girls' clubs, family vacations, a car at sixteen, and full financial support for college. My friends were always welcomed in our home, and although we were middle-income, I didn't grow up indulged like many of my peers. My parents set high standards for me, academically, morally, and even physically. They often said, "We know you come from good stock!" And I always believed that to be true (which only fueled my growing curiosity).

As I reflect back, the most difficult social situation for me was the annual family reunion we attended every August. My dad's side of the family was comprised of kind, highly educated, formal *side-huggers*. Although I enjoyed spending time with my cousins, it was subtly clear that bloodline and genetics carried a significant level of importance. Plus, my brother and I were the only adopted kids. My mom's side of the family always felt different. Chain-smoking farmers, full-on huggers, and the best cooks, they didn't seem to regard my adoption as an issue. When Mom told my grandmother they were going to adopt me, Grandmother shared honestly, "I don't know if I'll be able to love a child who isn't from blood."

But love proved deeper than blood. She and I became the best of friends, and I became her *favorite* (out of over forty grandchildren and great-grandchildren). Grandmother had an 8th-grade education, dipped snuff, was the best listener, and never judged me. She gave me time and acceptance in abundance.

The unique curious reality for the adoptee is a sense of *home*, of *place*. Every external need can be met, every emotional need attended to, and every necessary comfort made available, but there is a deep inner wonder. Questions always remained:

- Would I have been loved by my birth parents?

- Whose eyes do I have?

- Did I get my personality from my birth mom or my birth dad?

- Do they think of me?

One of my favorite childhood sitcoms was *I Dream of Jeannie*. Barbara Eden's almond-shaped eyes and bubbly demeanor drew me to her. My fantasy for years was that she was my birth mother. It still makes me smile thinking back on it today.

By the time I was eighteen and legally old enough to initiate a search, I had repeated an almost identical story to Kathy and Tom's. A romance led to a conception out of wedlock my freshman year of college. The difference was my boyfriend and I had dated for over a year, yet I had broken it off, knowing he wasn't the forever partner I was seeking. My parents were so disappointed in me, especially Mom.

Abortion was never a consideration. A counselor came to the house and tried to encourage me toward adoption. Deep down, I knew I couldn't do it. So, I finished the freshman semester. My new college friends slowly backed away as my belly grew. The rejection and shame were more than I could even begin to understand; I just swallowed it down. That year, 1984, became a massively lonely time. I married Mark and gave birth to our sweet-tempered eight-pound ten-ounce son, Jay. Even given Mom's heartache over my pregnancy, Jay became her favorite. Love wins again.

Mark and I divorced less than three years later. I married Mike, who welcomed Jay as his own. Our *blended family* moved to Saint Louis, Missouri, for Mike to eventually become a minister in the United Methodist Church. I worked full-time to support us, and a long journey of infertility began.

The Friday before Mother's Day, 1993, I received certified mail from the Department of Social Services. An immediate twinge danced in my belly, and I began to shake, opening the letter. In November 1992, I had petitioned the court to begin the search. It took six months. As Mom had encouraged over and over, it will either be a *yes* or a *no*. I was twenty-six years old.

The letter said, "The Department has contacted your birth mother, and she is quite anxious to have contact with you."

Quite anxious.

After two decades of wondering, imagining, rehearsing my response for either yes or no, she was *quite anxious.* It was just two days before Mother's Day, and there was her name, address, and phone number on a single sheet of paper in front of me. It was the central piece of my life puzzle, right there in my hands.

On Mother's Day afternoon, around 2 p.m., I called her. Few experiences in my fifty-four years have made me as nervous as that phone call. Kathy's mom, Nan, answered. Instinctively, Nan knew. Kathy and I had our first conversation just shortly after. I had a script nailed down. Given my teen pregnancy, I imagined her feelings. It was especially important to me that I validate her decision.

Clumsily, sweating, I blurted out, "I want you to know that I've had a good life. Thank you for saying yes to being contacted by me. I have been waiting a long time, and I would love to hear the whole story, exactly as it happened."

Time is a mystery. It seemed like we were on the phone for almost two hours, but it was likely only an hour. There were moments of easy exchange followed by stretches of silences. I had many questions, and Kathy made every effort to offer the details surrounding my birth, as well as share about her own life. The honesty I admire most from Kathy that day (and the hardest for me to hear) was when she said, "I considered abortion, but it wasn't legal in Kentucky."

Crickets.

Raw truth, not intended to hurt. A truth that was invited by me. And the truth that I had compassion for, having been faced with the exact same choice. To this day, I am profoundly grateful for the Kentucky laws against abortion in 1966.

We ended the call with a mutual enthusiasm to meet and agreed to exchange photos through the mail in the meantime.

Just a few days later, Mike called me at work. He had come home early, opened the mail from Kathy, and said, "You are not going to believe the resemblance!" There were the almond eyes (and the bubbly demeanor). Two weeks later, Mike, Jay, and I flew to Fort Myers, Florida, to meet for the first time and spend Memorial Day weekend with Kathy's family.

As our plane touched down, I began to wonder if other adoptees meeting their biological family for the first time have felt the same pressures of preparedness that I did. I have a history of over-functioning, and I certainly did for that visit. I had my hair done in a way I didn't normally wear but thought it would make an especially elegant first impression. Nails were perfect. Attempted to dress smart. Even dieted the days leading up to our trip.

Deep down, we adoptees are asking the questions, *Am I acceptable to you? Are you pleased? Maybe even proud?* Today, I would be much more comfortable in my own skin, but I masked a lot of insecurity at twenty-six.

After stepping off the plane, we collected our bags and were making our way to the exit when I saw her coming around the corner. There she was. There they were.

Kathy wore a regal Kelly-green dress. Stunning hair. Beautiful wide smile. So pretty! She was forty-six. We embraced—and held on. I have no words to accurately describe all that I felt at that moment. Kathy's younger daughter, Jennifer and her newborn son, Kathy's boyfriend, Kathy's mom Nan, Kathy's sister Andy, and others were all there with a warm and enthusiastic welcome.

Riding to Kathy's home, we sat side by side, casually observing each other, yet trying not to land in a full-on stare.

The *Ghost Kingdom* describes a theory often used by therapists when working with adoption cases.

B. J. Lifton, author, adoption counselor, and lecturer,

explains, "Therapists often ask me to supervise their work with adopted patients. I try to make the adoptee visible to them and to do this, I call in the ghosts that accompany everyone in the triad."

Adoptee

- On one side of the adoptee is the ghost of the child he/she might have been had he/she stayed with his/her birth mother.

- On the other side is the ghost of the child his/her adoptive parents might have had or the child who died. This ghost is like a sibling rival, whom the adoptee may try to compete with or give up on without even trying.

- And there is the ghost of the birth mother, from whom the adoptee has never fully disconnected, the ghost of the birth father, and the birth clan.

Birth mother

- The birth mother is accompanied by the ghost of the baby she gave up;

- The ghost of the birth father, who is gone;

- The ghost of the mother she might have been;

- The ghost of the adoptive parents who are raising

her child.

Adoptive Parents

- The adoptive parents are shadowed by the ghost of the perfect child they might have had;

- The ghost of the birth mother and birth father, whose child they are raising.

For me, the *Ghost Kingdom* was the imagined life with Kathy and Tom. A construct. A story created in my psyche. I imagined the three of us, riding in a car on a summer day with the windows rolled down and music on, me in the middle. Simple, free, and happy.

For Kathy, she'd always looked for me in crowds and places like Disney World.

Now, face to face, the *Ghost Kingdom* was confronted; a passionate pursuit of nature vs. nurture took flight, and the additional puzzle pieces of my life started fitting together. I have Kathy's hair, similar slim legs, and a familiar, feminine laugh.

Arriving at her home, a spread of food awaited us. She changed out of her sharp Kelly green and into shorts and a t-shirt that better suited her attractive form and elegant-casual style/personality. Turns out, we both may have over-functioned that day.

I took note of every detail she had poured into making the weekend spectacular until it was time to depart. Saying goodbye at the airport, Kathy imparted some personal words of encouragement meant only for the two of us. As I took my seat, I felt the dam break; I cried the entire flight home. Literally. Expression held back for twenty-six years. A range of emotions, finding necessary release. Exhausted and grateful.

In the years since, Kathy and I have navigated a relationship that is now closer than ever. We have sat together in her home until late at night, saying the words, tears streaming down our cheeks. We have lingered by her pool, sharing food and laughs. We have talked about recipes, parenting, health, and education. The writing of this story marks the 28th anniversary of my *reunion* with Kathy. One of her considerate, consistent efforts has been to speak respectfully and positively of my father, Tom. Many times, I have seen a glimmer in her eye when she's spoken of him. With sincerity, she wanted me to know him and him to know me. And, she had demonstrated a subtle protectiveness, hoping it would all unfold smoothly.

Kathy shared all that she knew about Tom, gave me her favorite photo of him, and even did a little innocent internet stalking to find out where he lived and what he did professionally. She shared the information she had gathered, should I desire to reach out. On an occasional basis, I looked him up. Years later, I even went so far as to call his home phone and hang up when the answer machine message was almost over, just to listen to the nuance of his deep voice.

After a seven-year journey of infertility, on September 5, 2001, I gave birth to Samuel, a long-awaited son. The following year on a beautiful, sunny Saturday in June, Mike and I went to a Saint Louis Cardinals baseball game and took baby Sam along. It was a happy day. But that night, as Mike was putting the final touches on his sermon and I was cleaning the kitchen counter from dinner, out of nowhere, I collapsed with chest pain that felt like the ram of a locomotive. Mike immediately called for an ambulance.

When we arrived at the ER, the doctor said the first responders likely did not get the heart monitor on me fast enough, so he wanted to run additional tests. I was released soon after and immediately sought out the top cardiologist in Saint Louis. She was a warrior for women's health, making known that heart disease is the number one killer of women in North America. I was thirty-five, healthy, active, and genuinely concerned.

Finally, I had an undeniable reason to call Tom. For years, my fear of rejection had kept me from ever leaving a message on his answering machine or calling him at work. Instinctively, I assumed that a birth *mother* would be reasonably more open to contact than a birth *father.* The *Ghost Kingdom* I imagined was that he was married to a lovely woman, had two and a half kids, and had a beautiful home with a spacious fenced yard. And without negative feelings, I thought it quite reasonable that his family would have known nothing about me.

Having learned he was a successful attorney, I also imagined he would reply with a well-worded and gracious *no*. I soon learned that couldn't have been further from the truth. On a summer night in early July, I finally summoned the courage to call, hoping he'd be home from work. His wife answered. Thinking back to that first phone call to Kathy again, with sweaty palms, I asked, "Is Tom available? My name is Dede, and I have reason to believe I am his biological daughter, born in 1966. I've had a recent scare with my health and am seeking to know more about family health history." She was kind and responded with, "Tom is in San Francisco on business, but I'm sure he will be very interested to know you have called and will be eager to be in touch with you."

Heart palpitations. I heard, "Quite anxious." Or maybe that was my desire taking over.

The next afternoon, Sam and I were playing in the backyard baby pool when the phone rang. It was Tom. As he started to speak, I could hardly believe I was finally going to have an actual conversation with the voice on the answering machine. Interestingly, his first words were, "Dede, this is Tom. Are you mad at me?" Surprised, I answered, "No." With compassion, I gradually began to consider his feelings. Had he carried this ghost around for three decades? A daughter that was angry?

As to health history, Tom had a stent placed that very April. He shared with me that there were significant heart issues in his family. He flew to Saint Louis the following

115

month to meet me. Again, the over-functioning impulsive-ness kicked in, and I deliberated on what to wear, my hair, nails, etc. When we agreed to meet at his hotel lobby, I asked, "How will you know me?" He responded, "Just walk in, and I'll know." That's exactly how it happened. The tall, dark, and handsome was right in front of me. He was a gracious gentleman, dressed impeccably, listened well, and was quite easy to talk to.

We enjoyed an Italian dinner, and when he walked me to my car, we shared an embrace. A similar holding on that I had experienced with Kathy that sunny morning in the airport. Again, it's impossible for me to fully express the emotions of being with the one whose same blood flows through my veins for the first time.

This year Tom and I will celebrate twenty years of knowing each other. Our relationship has grown into a sweet union of friendship, trust, and celebration of our common personalities, many shared preferences, and the discovery that we are both introverts. Physically, we have the same smile, same hands, and even the same *backsides*, not much in the buttocks, a truth we've belly-laughed about. We enjoy long walks with our dogs, shared meals, and meaningful conversations. Tom has demonstrated through the years that he was quite anxious to know me. Turns out, I am his only offspring.

Life learner that I am, I've read many books written by experts on this subject and sought to understand the deep-er, hidden aspects of a story such as ours. Among the most compelling was a study conducted by a team of neurobiol-ogists. The team contacted large hospitals in Los Angeles, New York, and Boston, announcing they'd be visiting the maternity wards and not to make any changes in the way the infants were arranged in nurseries. In other words, they did not want the nurses to separate the babies being relin-quished for adoption from the others.

The goal of the trial was for the doctors to try and dis-tinguish *from the cries alone* the babies being relinquished. The team was 100 percent accurate. The conclusion: the adoptees' life begins with grief, based on a primal quality in the cry. Grief has been among the primary shared emotions that Kathy, Tom, and I have experienced. I would add to that: shame, confusion, sadness, joy, relief, gratitude, de-light, and happiness.

I consider the words we've used around our unique sto-ries:

"gave up"

"relinquished"

"unwed"

"rejection"

"abandonment"

"loss"

As significant as language and image have become in our culture, around race, gender, and equal rights, I wonder if these terms no longer fit. How might we curate language with deeper sensitivity that still conveys the truth of our stories?

My personal study, personal therapy, and maturation have helped me understand that through the years, I created my own suffering by occasionally placing unrealistic expectations around some aspects of our relationship. I've learned that allowing each relationship to grow, flourish and become beautiful in its own organic way, covers everyone in a warm embrace of grace.

This is my honest confession, with a peaceful, settled heart, that everything in my life turned out as it was meant to be. I am fully aware that mine is a life of abundance. I am doubly blessed to have a relationship with everyone involved in the story.

All along, I was quite anxious to know Kathy and Tom. I simply cannot conceive of my life without them in it. How I love the *nature* I possess from them!

And always, I am deeply grateful for the commitment, love, support, and *nurture* I received from Mom and Dad.

Love wins again.

Kathy

I have not yet had the privilege of meeting Kathy. She shared her story with me through Dede. Like me and so many others, Kathy needed to make a difficult choice at a young age. I hope one day to meet Kathy in person and thank her for sharing with us.

Kathy's Story, Birth Mom "God's Gift of Choices"

I found that I was pregnant in my first year of college and feared the thought of raising a child when I did not have a job or even an education to get a job. My mother told me that she would help me in whatever I decided to do. She took me to an unwed mothers' home in a nearby town as the shame of being unmarried and pregnant was not conducive to staying at home. It had bars on the windows, and that seemed like a dismal place to be. I have a cousin who was adopted, and I asked to visit with the lady who arranged that adoption, and she explained the choice was mine to make and to consider it carefully. She told me that when papers are signed, that I would not be allowed to try to find the child later, but if the child wanted to find me, they would disclose the information to help find me.

I moved in with my aunt and uncle, who lived in another city far away, and stayed with them during the last three months of the pregnancy. Then on October 5, 1966, labor pains began, and I was taken to hospital, had a spinal block, and do not even remember the pain after that. I had been told that I would not get to see the baby, but someone brought her to me for a while, and Mother took a picture. I named her Alicia. I held her for a while, and then they took her away forever to meet her new family.

I thought about her constantly and even tried to contact the father as the only way to get her back would be to go through the adoption process. Not likely that we would qualify, and they already had a happy family who had taken her. Many years went by, and I would always think October 5 was a special day for me as well as being her birthday.

Life went on, and I was married and divorced two times and finally had another baby on January 1, 1974. I wondered each day when I looked at how happy and healthy this new baby was whether the one I let go of was just as healthy and happy.

In March 1993, I received a call from a social worker who asked me if I had a child who was born on October 5, 1966. I said, "Yes," and she said, "Would you be okay with me giving her your contact info? She would like to contact you." As I caught my breath, I said, "Yes." Days went by, and I wondered about this call. Finally, on Mother's Day in 1993, I got that call from Dede, who said she was that child! What joy I felt getting that call and being able to ask about her life and health and family. I was so happy to hear she was adopted by a loving couple in Hopkinsville who named her Deandra Dawn, and that they also adopted another child, so she had a brother, and then later they had a child, so she had a sister too. We shared pictures and, of course, were amazed at the resemblance, also amazed that my niece and nephew, who lived in Hopkinsville, knew her in high school (not close friends, but they knew who she was). It is a small world, and I wanted so much to see and feel her; she was agreeable to make the trip to Florida to meet my family, and my family was just as eager to meet her. My sister came down from Kentucky, and my mother lives with me. My daughter JJ was here as she'd just had her first child, Rusty, so this huge entourage headed to the airport for this reunion.

Dede, Mike, and Jay (who was six) came down the aisle like a bridal procession, and we rushed to each other in a long-awaited embrace which has been captured in a photo that Dede framed and sent to me. I pass by that picture every day on the way to my bedroom.

The acceptance of each other seemed to be unanimous, and the years of shame that I had endured were gone in a flash. I had been shamed for getting pregnant outside of marriage and had spent twenty-seven years worrying about her upbringing only to find that she had no hard feelings for my *giving her up*. I was never able to say that until this day; I always said, "She was adopted," as that seemed nicer than "I gave her up." I gave her up to have a better life than I could have given her.

Our relationship since that day has grown even stronger, and we may go for a while with no contact and then just *pick back up* where we left off and catch up. I think we have that connection that all mothers have with their children; after all, a part of my body is that body, and we will always be connected even if we do not connect every day.

I was truly fortunate to get to visit with her adoptive parents, and they shared stories and pictures of her life events. That filled in the gaps, and I am so thankful for that experience and their willingness to share.

Life is full of *choices*, and sometimes we must go with our heart's desire, and other times, it is best to do what is best for all involved. *Choice* is just one of the gifts God gives us. And I am so happy that Dede chose to reconnect with me in 1993.

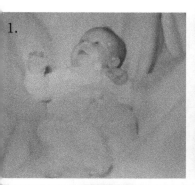

1. Dede's Home-coming
2. Dede and Kathy, her birth mom, meeting for the first time
3. Dede and Kathy 2021
4. Dede and Tom, her birth dad

Josiah, Tabitha, and Eliza

Tina (their mom) and I met at our church through MOPS (Mothers of Preschoolers). I was volunteering to watch the kids while the moms had their meetings. Tina brought Tabitha to those meetings, so I got to look after her when she was just a baby. I also helped a ladies' Bible study group and watched their kids, which Tina was part of too. I didn't know her story back then. Again, God was bringing people into my life that would someday play a role I couldn't imagine. Hers is a beautiful story of how God built her family and of her obedience to Him. I am happy to include brief comments from Tabitha, age ten, here. Her son, Josiah, age seventeen, decided not to participate because he is still processing his feelings regarding his adoption.

Tabitha's Story

Adoption is great, and I always wanted a little sister, and I got what I wanted. It makes me feel special, and I love my home. It's great here. I love my family and my friends. And I have a school I love.

Adoption is amazing. It is okay to be adopted. It is okay to miss your birth family. My birth mom Evelyn is special to me, and I miss her. Maybe one day I might want to see her. *God is for you and me!*

Tina's Story, Adoptive Mom

"I praise you because I am fearfully and wonderfully made; your works are wonderful; I know that full well" (Psalm 139:14).

I was twenty-five years old before I knew that I was fearfully and wonderfully made. I am a constant learner of His wonderful works, and I am still striving to know that full well. One of the greatest revelations of my life is the unconditional love God has for me. It is that love and saving faith in Jesus Christ that moved me to love beyond myself and to love more than I ever imagined possible. When I experienced the unconditional love of Christ, something inside me longed to share that love with others. My firstborn, Zachary (whom God remembered), was birthed from that desire to love. He is my *love* child. I prayed for a baby, and months later, he was conceived. I carried him in my womb for nine months with all the love I had. Jeff and I were thrilled to welcome him into our lives; Zachary is wonderfully made.

It was ten years later when I heard God speak to me, declaring, "You will adopt a daughter, Tabitha." "In Greek, her name is Dorcas (meaning gazelle)" (Acts 9:36). Although I had grown content with my little family, I was *all in*, desiring to follow whatever road Jesus had put before me. I did remind God that He would have to inform my husband Jeff of this surprising news. God did, in His incredible and extraordinary way. As Jeff and I were scouring the local newspaper for real estate agents to sell our home, Jeff pointed to the name of a local agent, Dorcas, and verbally asked, "Who would name their child Dorcas?" It was the open door I needed to explain to Jeff what God had whispered to me. I swelled with joy as this baby was conceived in my heart. Jeff, too, was *all in*, and Tabitha took a prominent place at the top of my prayer list. Within three years, the nursery was painted pink, and the flowered ceiling fan was hung. We presented our adoption book to a birthmother. I joyfully waited. To my dismay, the birth mother did not choose us. I felt rejection, but God's word reminded me that "Ye have not chosen me, but I have chosen you" (John 15:16, KJV). I believed in my heart that our baby would be home by Christmas, taking on the quickness of a gazelle. On a cold rainy December, as I stood in church, thinking I had missed God and misunderstood His plan, I felt defeated, and my joy turned to sorrow. The emotional roller coaster was wreaking havoc in my mind until a friend in Christ shared a word with me, reminding me that "What God has spoken, will always come to pass" (Ezekiel 24:14, paraphrased by the author). As the winter days drew colder and darker, my joy faltered. It would be days into the new year before we received a phone call from the adoption agency. The baby born to the birthmother that did not originally choose us was needing a new placement. The agency was seeking a new home for this now six-week-old baby. Jeff and I took the weekend to pray, but I never doubted that this was our child. Josiah (found by God), who was born in December, the weekend I thought I misunderstood God's plan, came home forty days after his birth. He was home in his pink room with his flowered ceiling fan, and we knew God's hand was moving. When birthmother Barbara placed Josiah in our arms, my joy was restored. Barbara has a place in my heart that is more precious than I can express. I see her in Josiah's eyes. He has her facial features and her hands. She is a strong woman who chose to carry Josiah against the world's way and make a plan for him to be loved. She is one of the least selfish. I anticipate a day when Josiah and Barbara can meet. I know that day will bring a range of emotions, and joy will fill them both. He is my *joy* baby. Josiah is wonderfully made.

But God said, "You will adopt Tabitha," and I became well aware that the adoption journey would continue. Two years later, while filling out adoption papers, I became pregnant. I admit I cried for two weeks. I was forty-one years old and shocked and confused. I did not think this was the plan; it was not my plan. "I know the plans I have for you, declares the Lord, plans to prosper you and not to harm you, plans to give you hope and a future" (Jeremiah 29:11). My mother's intuition took over, and I knew that I was carrying a baby boy. In my daily prayers and conversations with God, I was given peace. The peace that I needed to carry this baby boy. In the third trimester of my pregnancy, my baby was diagnosed with a heart condition. Under an abundance of medical care, Jeremiah (God will raise up) was born. He was the baby that drove me to God's peace, "A peace that surpasses all understanding" (Phillipians 4:7, paraphrased by the author) and "A peace in the midst of the storm" (John 14:27, paraphrased by the author). Through excellent medical care and a miraculous surgery, Jeremiah's heart was healed, and I was taught that "Perfect peace comes when my mind is steadfast, and I trust in Jesus" (Isaiah 26:3, KJV). He is my *peace* baby—Jeremiah is wonderfully made.

With her name, Tabitha, still stirring in my heart, Jeff and I were led to begin fostering for the state. I must admit that I continually looked for Tabitha in the eyes of all the children that we cared for. After two years of fostering and on the heels of a yearly spiritual fast, I received a phone call from the state. A newborn baby girl was placed in care, and an adoption plan would soon be made. I knew at that moment that Tabitha was coming home. I pulled the car to the side of the road and wept. Hope was now dancing in my heart. It would be two and a half years of fostering her before our adoption was finalized, but I remained hopeful through all of the emotional chaos. "Hope deferred makes the heart sick; but a longing fulfilled is a tree of life" (Proverbs 13:12). For ten years, I had prayed and hoped for Tabitha. She is my *hope* baby—Tabitha is wonderfully made.

Believing our family was now complete and the promises of God were fulfilled, Jeff and I relinquished our foster licenses and settled into our family of six. Eight years later, on a September evening, I received a phone call from the state. I was told that a baby girl had come into care, and she was the biological sister of Tabitha. My heart melted. I presented the news to Jeff, and his heart melted too. We both knew that God was calling us to adopt this sister and welcome her into our home. It was a struggle for me. I was older, and I had developed my own ways and thoughts about my future. "As the heavens are higher than the earth, so are my ways higher than your ways and my thoughts than your thoughts" (Isaiah 55:9). God, in His goodness, gave me much grace and allowed me the space to engage all the various emotions I had. "Don't be afraid; just believe" (Mark 5:36). We brought our daughter home to her family, and Tabitha named her Eliza (pledged to God). She is my *believe* baby—Eliza is wonderfully made.

Our adoption story is one that I could have never imagined, but it is the story that God has written in each of our lives. As an adoptive mother, I ponder if I am enough for my children. I question if I will have the right answers for them. My heart hurts for them, for their loss, for their grief, and their wondering. I pray continually for their birth mothers and birth fathers. I pray that one day they may meet to see whose eyes they have, whose personality they most portray and whose mannerisms they display.

More often than not, I have no answers for them except, "You are fearfully and wonderfully made."

"Now to Him who is able to do immeasurably more than all we ask or imagine, according to his power that is at work within us, to Him be glory in the church and in Jesus Christ throughout all generations, forever and ever! Amen" (Ephesians 3:20-21).

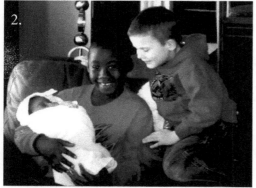

1. Josiah's homecoming
2. Tabitha's homecoming with her two big brothers
3. Family photo
4. Tabitha and her sister Eliza

Nicholas

Elizabeth and Bradley

This couple was introduced to me through a new friend I met in a writers' group. They have asked to remain anonymous; their names have been changed for privacy. I was unfortunately not able to speak with Nicholas. His mom's story appears here. This family has quite a beautiful and tragic history of adoptions through several generations. They were strangers who graciously opened their hearts to share their family's story with the hope it will benefit others. Adoption is beautiful, joy-filled, loving, and courageous. It is also tragic, heart-breaking, and just plain hard. This family has experienced all of this. It is certainly not unique to them. Although I have not yet met them in person, their story touched my heart, and I know you will feel the same.

Elizabeth's Story, Adoptive Mom

As a family, we cover the adoption triad. My (Elizabeth's) mother was adopted as an infant in 1941 and, I believe she suffers from reactive attachment disorder to this day. This has never been diagnosed, nor was it even a diagnosis when she was a child.

I grew up never knowing my birth father because he and my mother were divorced when I was only two and a half years old. I was allowed to keep two photographs of him. When they divorced, Mother moved us from Seattle to Washington, DC. My mother remarried when I was five years old, and my stepfather adopted me. Unfortunately, this marriage ended with a very ugly divorce when I was nineteen. I was forced to take my mother's *side* and never spoke to my adoptive stepfather again from the age of eighteen on. My father was awarded custody of my younger half-sister in the divorce. My sister and I became close as adults but are currently estranged.

When I was fourteen, my family moved back to the Seattle area. One of the first things I did when we arrived on the west coast was look up my biological father in the phone book. I was glad to know he was alive, but I was scared to contact him. I knew that contacting him would be very upsetting to my mother, so I never told her and never reached out to my biological father. To this day, she harbors hatred toward him. I cannot fathom holding onto such bitterness over a relationship of fewer than four years, over fifty years in the past. It was such a long time ago.

When I was in my late 20s, my biological father contacted my maternal grandparents to find me. They passed along his phone number to me. I called him right away. It was an easy decision for me, and I did not tell my mother about reconnecting with him. My husband and I drove across the state to meet my father for the first time at a restaurant in Seattle. I had no recollection of him from my early years. So many things finally made sense. I look nothing like my mother or sister and but so much like my father. My body shape, nose, eyebrows, sense of humor, and talent with a camera mirrored my father. I learned that his sister shared the same infertility issues with me and that a first cousin and I were married the same weekend in nearly the same wedding dress. He attended her wedding on Long Island the same weekend I was married in the Seattle area.

My husband's parents were pregnant before marriage with his brother in the early 1960s. They were both teenagers, and marriage was the only acceptable option at the time. Within two years, my husband was born. His mother became pregnant with a third child, and she moved with the boys to her parents' home in another state. The two boys had no recollection of this pregnancy and move because they were so young. Their mother made her parents tell everyone the baby died at birth when in reality, she placed the baby for adoption. The boys grew up not knowing they had a biological sister. It was a deeply kept secret. Within three years of his birth, my husband's parents divorced. Their hatred for each other was palpable as the boys grew up. They did get to see their father during summer break.

My husband and his brother were reunited with their younger sister when they were in their thirties. They found out, ironically, that she grew up in a happy home with two older brothers. Their mother did reunite with the daughter she placed for adoption, but their relationship was strained and is essentially nonexistent.

I met my husband when we were fifteen years old and attending high school together. We were engaged at age twenty and married at twenty-three after we both received our bachelor's degrees. After our wedding, I went on to earn my master's degree, and we bought a home. As a young married couple, we felt an overwhelming desire to become parents. I suffered from PCOS, and we both dealt with heart-wrenching infertility. It was the early 1990s, and although we both had jobs, our health insurance did not cover infertility treatments. We decided to adopt to fulfill our dream of being parents. We explored adopting from several foreign countries. We were rejected by one because of my weight, and we rejected others because of the exorbitant costs involved. Our home study social worker connected us with an agency in Washington, DC. We endured the intrusive, stressful, and incredibly challenging vetting process, which took six months. The ache we felt for a child of our own overshadowing all of it. I will never forget the pages of named disabilities that we had to review. Would we accept a blind child? A child with a missing limb? A child with an intellectual disability? A baby with AIDS? Was it wrong for us to just want what any other pregnant couple would wish for, a healthy baby? We decided that we would accept a healthy baby, and like any other parents, would love and accept whatever issues came along as the child grew.

Our search ended with the birth of an African American baby boy. We learned of him when he was five days old. He was placed with a foster family for the three weeks it took for the birth mother's rights to be terminated and the interstate compact to be developed. I spoke daily with his foster family during the time they had him until he was flown across the country and into our arms.

Our son was such a happy baby and sweet toddler. Researching the challenges of inter-racial adoption, we strove to expose our son to his African American culture as much as possible while living in a very Caucasian city. Fortunately, we have a close friend who became another grandmother for our son and welcomed him into her family. Our son was able to spend time as a teenager with her family in the summer after they moved to Mississippi.

Our son's struggles first manifested with learning disabilities when he was in the third grade. His life really fell apart as he entered puberty and junior high school. As parents, we were strict but also gave him the freedom and independence to hang out with friends. Unfortunately, this was the opposite of what he needed from us. We are the parents of a special needs child, but we didn't know about his diagnosis until he was seventeen. Our son has Fetal Alcohol Spectrum Disorder (FASD). He has a normal IQ, but his executive functioning is developmentally delayed due to the brain damage he suffered in utero when his birth mother drank alcohol. In learning about FASD, we learned in hindsight that we should not have given him the same freedoms as typically developing teenagers. He would have benefited from a very structured environment sheltered from the influence of others.

Our son's birth mother chose a closed adoption. She has never reached out to the agency to contact our son. I tried to reach out to her but received no reply. As a young child, our son told us that he remembered hearing his siblings' voices, and we know his birth mother had two older children in the home when she was pregnant. Maybe one day, he will search for his siblings. Our son is twenty-six years old now and living with us in our home along with his daughter, of whom he recently was awarded 50 percent custody. He has had several different jobs after graduating high school, along with periods of unemployment, drug use, and felonies. He dreams of community college, which is a possibility after he pays off debts. He is currently working and, despite his challenges, is a devoted and loving father. Having that biological connection to his daughter means everything to him. He has made significant positive changes in his life because of her.

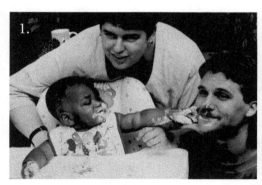

1. Elizabeth, Bradley and Nicholas
2. Nicholas and his daughter
3. Nicholas and his grandfather

22

JJ is one of those *divine appointments*. While seeking out a volunteer opportunity, I struck up a conversation with another woman volunteering alongside me. I mentioned my story to her and my desire to find men willing to tell their stories for this book. She immediately thought of JJ. They attend church together and are good friends. JJ and his wife, Lori, were very receptive to sharing his story with us. JJ has an exuberant faith, and it shows up in every conversation with him. After our first phone call, it felt as if we'd been friends forever! I knew it was vital to share a man's voice so that perhaps other men, who may be hesitant for whatever reasons, will find a way to talk about their adoption story.

JJ's Story

I grew up in a country home in Peru, New York, which is near Plattsburgh airbase, in apple orchard country. My dad was a WWII veteran. He is my absolute flipping hero on this planet, except now, he's in heaven. He was a general contractor after returning from WWII, and his claim to fame was that his company built cold storage for these huge apple orchards. These orchards could now store apples for the first time late into the season; they could keep apples fresh for grocery stores where previously they weren't able to do that for long periods.

My big life-changing event came through my sister. She was adopted before me. She's two and a half years older than me and not of the same blood. She was adopted first, and I think she was over a year old when Mom and Dad adopted her. I am told we both came from the Lund Home up in Vermont. When they started the process on me, they already had my sister, and I was a dream yet to be fulfilled. They knew that I was yet to come into this world. I arrived, and they got me *off the showroom floor.*

In 1966, close to my 3rd birthday, we arrived in New Mexico. We moved there because of my dad's arthritis. I remember the moment vividly! My sister and I were downstairs in the basement playing. (I kid around about it, but she was always the *mean green jellybean big sister.* She could pound on me, and I would do whatever she'd said.) And she said, "John, guess what?" "What?" I said, and she said, "We're adopted." So, I said, "What's adopted mean?" I remember it as it happened a minute ago. She says, "Mommy and Daddy are not our real Mommy and Daddy." Like I was supposed to understand that as an insult. I puffed up big, and I said, "Mommy and Daddy are our Mommy and Daddy!" Then, I went stomping up the stairs right into the kitchen. My mom was in the kitchen, and she turned around and said, "Well, what's the matter here?" And I stomped up to her, and looking up; I said, "Mommy, Harriet said you and Daddy are not our real Mommy and Daddy." Mom picked me up, and she put me on her knee right at the kitchen table. I don't remember what she said to me, exactly, but I remember her telling me something like,

"No. Now, your mom couldn't keep you. But Daddy and I love you, and we are your Mommy and Daddy." Whatever she said was exactly perfect for me to hear in my little three-year-old heart. That's all I needed, and I'm good to go. To me, I am the same guy inside right now that I was at three years old. As far as I'm concerned, the Spirit God breathed into all of us, it's that same one we grow and nurture, and that is the true me. Something in me said, "Okay, watch how this goes because it's my will."

We grew up in a loving, Christian, modest, conservative home. Work, discipline, responsibility, the name that you wear, and who you're going to become are a big deal. The words out of your mouth matter. You're going to respect Mom and Dad not because that's what I said but because that's what we do. I wasn't quite ten years old when my sister began running away, which made her about twelve years old. The first time she ran away, she just wasn't where she was supposed to be. This became a now and then occurrence. Then it got to a point where she'd be gone for longer periods. The big deal happened when I was thirteen, and she came out into the den where Dad and I were playing pool. My dad, despite his arthritis, still built things, and our house was a lot bigger than it was, to begin with, because of his craftsmanship and love. The den used to be the garage. My sister comes to the doorway, and she asked, "John, what do you think of this?" She had on this dress she made. And again, remember I'm thirteen, I said, "Well, I don't know it kind of makes you look like you're pregnant." She blew a gasket and stormed off. My dad looked at me and just shook his head and shrugged, "Oh well," and we continue our pool game. She ran away that night, and I never saw her again until between my freshman and sophomore years of junior college. By then, I'm taller than her, which wasn't the norm; she was always eight inches taller and hundred pounds heavier than me. All that is to say, although we grew up in the same home of love and faith and grace and dignity and honor, we're not of the same character; our hearts were not the same at all.

Whenever I would ask as I'm growing up, my mom and dad would both tell me, "Your mom was a farm girl raised in faith and grace and just simply could not have you stay." They were correct about a lot of what they thought they knew. My sister, on the other hand, to the degree they cared for me to know about her; they would say only that she was already a little bit older when they got her, and they said they knew something about her mom.

When we found my mom, it prompted my sister to really try to find her mom, and everything she thought or had heard was, in fact, true. She was just wild at heart, not rooted or grounded. My sister found out that she had siblings that were in prison, like everything of that lineage followed in that same unfortunate path. In my mom's lineage, there's grace, faith, and devotion to family. It seems to me that blood is a lot stronger than just the environment that you grew up in because we grew up in the same environment. We were from different worlds, and we proved it.

In my world, the only way to define your history was

through the family photo album. When you're a little kid, it's just so cool to look at the family photos. My dad, a WWII 8th Air Force veteran, was a very soft-spoken man. He had all these WWII photographs and mementos, and I'd look through them and think, *That's my dad! Wow!* I went to a military school. That experience made a large impact on who I am. I was fourteen when I started, five feet six inches and 129 pounds ringing wet, and could still look my dad square in the eye. That was in August. Well, I didn't get to see Mom and Dad again until just before Thanksgiving. The school had all these big activities all happened at once, like homecoming and the talent show. Picture this, I came out into this long hallway, and look down to the opposite end and see Mom and Dad's car and then, wow, there's Dad and Mom standing there. I can't run; I've got to walk like I'm supposed to because this is a military school. So, I start making my way down there, and the closer I got, the more I thought, *What's going on?* I walked up and said, "Hi Dad." And I was looking down at him. This is weird. I've grown a lot in just a few months. My dad was all heart, and he'll always be a mountain of a man in my mind and heart. After military school, I came home for a year, and then I moved back to the town where the military school was, which is only 200 miles away. So, I'm living in Roswell. My sister, at long last, had returned and was living at the house with Mom and Dad. I'm home one weekend, and my sister calls and says you need to get up here right away because Dad has had a grand mal seizure. I have no idea what that is, so she tells me, and like a rocket, I made my way to Albuquerque. For about eleven days, twice a day every day, I spend two or two and a half hours with my dad up in his room at the hospital. And in that course of time, we probably went through everything that we had not said that we needed to say. We talked about life in those eleven days. He said, "Let me tell you something. You need to find your mom." I said, "I'm good. I know where I come from." To the degree he could squeeze a hand with his arthritic hands, he grabbed my hand, and he said, "No, you listen to me! Before she gets like this, you need to find your mom. You need to find out more about what happened." I said, "Only with your blessing. I'm not going to promise you that I will but to know that I can." I wasn't thinking about it at first, or even most of the way through, until they said that he's getting well. "Probably tomorrow he'd be released to come back home." On my way back down to Roswell, I'm thinking there's a lot of stuff to process here. I wonder what he was thinking; they're letting him out of the hospital. He can't be talking about the end of life. But I was only home a day and a half when my sister called again and said, "You've got to get back up here." I get up there, and he is actually on his deathbed. And every time he tried to talk, he couldn't. He would cough, and I might have heard three words from him. My mom had Alzheimer's, and from the time I was twelve years old, we watched it develop. Praise God, she was never violent, but she was forgetful and regressed into a little girl. My dad just had this amazingly loving way with her. They were lost without each other. My mom was Dad's body (because of his arthritis), and my dad was Mom's brain. They were inseparable. It was cool to take my mom over there to see my dad. I was getting ready to take my mom home. My dad always watched my mom real close, and he gave me a look that said, "You take care of her." The words busted out of me, "Dad, you're my hero." His eyes got big as though he understood. I said, "If you want to, Dad, in the morning, you get out of this bed, and I'll take you home. But if you want, you can go home tonight. You know, and I know where you'll go because we all know you're good. But I'm going to take Mom home, and I'll be back here shortly." My dad's two sisters lived next door to my mom, and they were rock solid. Many times, they'd already been in the hospital room talking to him, or I might take one or the other over. I left my mom at home; this was about 4:30 in the afternoon; and went back to the hospital, and both of my dad's sisters were there. They were getting ready to leave. They had no idea that I was coming back, and it was just coincidental, but I got back right when they're saying their goodbyes.

When I got back, he was looking at me differently. My dad said more with his heart and his eyes than he ever had to out of his mouth, and if you knew what you were look-ing at and listening to, you heard a lot of wisdom out of that man. Dad's favorite nurse was working that night and reas-sured us that she'd be watching him. My sister was friends with this nurse, so we knew if anything at all happened, she'd call. I was in kind of a "backslidden" time in my life just then, but if you're backslidden, that means you still have some faith inside you. That faith that's in there, the Word of God, doesn't get planted on your heart and leave; it's there. And God's love, Jesus' prevenient love, is so cool that He's all the time whispering, "Hey, come on, come on." As I lay down, amid all the stuff that's going on, I remember praying that night that Dad would be peaceful whatever is going to happen. I remember just thinking about how heavy everything was, but my thoughts were interrupted when the phone rang. I don't know what time it was, but my sister came walking in. It seemed like a half-hour, and it probably was five minutes, but she comes in, and she said, "Well, he's gone." She said that the nurse explained to her that some alarm happened on the monitors, and she went in to see my dad, and she held his hand. The nurse said she could see the light leave my dad, and she thought there he goes. Dad had already said what he wanted, how he wanted it done, who's going to be there and what's not going to happen. And so, it was a quiet little service. That was in 1989.

I meet my darlin', Lori. We fall madly in love, and we moved from New Mexico to Missouri because of my job. It's 1990 or 1991, and there are all these television shows about twins finding each other and adoption reunions. I don't know how many times we looked at each other and said, "You know, that's something to think about." Then one day, it just hit us that we ought to try. I knew that it was the Lund Home. Now there's no internet; it's the early '90s. So, it took a couple of phone calls, and sure enough, the Lund Home has changed its name, and there they are. Same place, same people. We call the number, this lady answers, and I'm just rattling off until she said, "Okay, let me stop for a second. Now here's what you need to do. I can't answer all your questions. I'm sorry, as much as I'd love to, I can't. You really need a search assistant." And I said, "Okay, you've let me go on and on this long to tell me that because you know a search assistant that maybe I could talk to, right?" She said, "Yes, as a matter of fact, I do." It turns out our search assistant and this lady at the home are best friends, but they are both very professional. We get connected with this lady, and she said, "I would be glad to be your search assistant, and here's what you need to do. First, I'm going to send you a book, and you need to read the book. Then send me half of my price, and I will start to search. When we make contact, and you guys are brought together, that's when you give me the other half. Whatever happens after that, that's on you. And if you want to let me know what happened, that's okay, but you don't have to." And it could not have been more wonderful. We started the search on September 15, 1991, and she would give us these little updates anywhere from one to three times a week. Things like "I found a letter in the last name." Some days, she said, "Okay, I need you to call back up there (to the Lund Home), and they will only answer yes or no questions. These are the following questions I want you to ask." And then the next time she would have us call, she'd say, "Okay, I want you to ask them this now." All this stuff's developing, and then, on the night before Thanksgiving, we speak, my mom who gave me life and me. I'm going to say for the second time because I got to hear that voice for nine months; I just couldn't remember it. This is before we have our girls, so every two or three weeks, we go home to Kansas to visit Lori's mom and dad. We're sharing with them everything that's going on, and every time we'd go over,

Lori's mom said, "Did you talk to your mom yet?" Our replies, "No, but here's what's going on right now." Or "No, but here's what they found out now." Lori's parents came to see us on Thanksgiving. When I talked with my mom, I was even telling her how Lori's mom and dad have been asking all this time if I got to talk to you. When they pull up in the driveway, it's about thirty yards from the house to where they parked, and the sun had gone down; Lori's mom gets out of the van, looks at me, and says, "You talked to your mom!" So, we got to talk the first time; then, we shared photos, letters, and phone calls for a long time.

She lives in Vermont. And, not that far from where I grew up or where my mom and dad that raised me are from and where their families are, so it seemed like something that we could do. From the family farm, it's only a three or four-hour drive to where Mama Liz lives. I don't know how that was arranged or planned, but God winked.

On Mother's Day of 1992, we spend a week in Vermont. Half with my mom that gave me birth and the other half at my godparent's farm, all arranged and coordinated by my favorite cousin, Linda (we somehow always remained in contact), putting this together with my darlin', Lori. It's just beyond magical. Since then, we have been tight, just tight at a distance. I don't want to be in their way. The last thing I would want to do is interfere or be any kind of a bother or nuisance. But I want to forever be a living, breathing, thank you card, and that's what I told them when we first talked. I said, "You know, Mama Liz, if there was anything I could say, it's 'thank you for life.' And if you never hear me say anything else or if you don't want to hear me say anything ever again. It doesn't matter, as long as you got to hear me say thank you for life because I'm alive." And she said, "Oh, you don't know what that means." Every time we talk, even now, at the beginning and the end and somewhere probably in the middle of it, I tell her thank you for life.

When we connected with Mama Liz, her mom was alive. Grandma, my mom (Mama Liz), and Papa Wayne (her husband and first love) live at the farmhouse. First, we met at this restaurant. We were there for over three and a half hours and thought we certainly are going to get kicked out of here. The lady kept bringing us iced tea and everything, saying, "I just keep wanting to hear, this is so cool. I want to hear more." Well, we know we're causing a stir, so we went out into the parking lot for a half-hour to talk out there, and then we finally get up to the farm. We're sitting there on the front porch at my grandma's house. Mom and Grandma are sitting on one side and Lori and I are sitting over on the other side. As we're talking, now and then, Grandma would smile, and she'd lean over and whisper something. And so finally, my mom said, "Gram just wanted me to let you know that when she hears you talk, you sound just like your grandpa, except with that funny accent." We all laughed at that! This is a funny happenstance: Mama Liz is in Vermont; their zip code is 05738. And she said, "I graduated in '57, and I was born in '38."

We were at the farm talking for I don't know how long until finally Grandma said she had to go to bed. Then Papa Wayne went to bed too. Now, it's just Lori, Mama Liz, and me, and she's telling us more and more. She waited until Lori and I were sitting with her, and she could look at me across the table right in the eye to say where I came from and how and why. Well, I'm a date rape. She lived on a dairy farm, and this fellow was raised on a feed grain farm that distributed feed grain to many of the neighboring dairy farms. My mom said that she knew this fellow, that they grew up together. He's older than her, but I don't know by how much. And anyway, she said they played together as kids, and they'd gone out together a few times with a group of friends. That night he'd asked her out on a date to the show. They weren't far from the house when she realized he had drunk a lot. She said, "He was going to have his way with me, and he's a bigger guy. What was I going to be able to do?" And that was just what happened. And she said, "I want you to know I knew right away I was pregnant. You're not supposed to know for weeks because they do a pregnancy test, but I knew. I want you to know, not for one second were you ever not going to be born." There aren't any accidents. I don't care what anybody says. She was twenty-one when I was born.

I'm not sure how far into the pregnancy she was when they met with the Lund Home, but Mama Liz explained how she developed such a wonderful relationship with the staff at the Lund Home that she had favor with them. They said, "You can tell no one what we're doing, or we could all be fired." They let her actually hold me. This is back in 1963. They took a whole roll of film. Those pictures are a treasure. She showed them to us, Lori and me, when we first met her. Photos of her holding me on her belly and holding me to her bosom just like any mom that just had a

baby would do. And she said, "You know, they could have
been fired if anybody would have known this happened."
She (Mama Liz) got to love on me like you're not supposed
to be able to. I know why it happened; because there's a
love inside of me, like maybe I'm not supposed to have.
And maybe I am supposed to have that love in there. There
were too many things that happened that were just too God,
not to acknowledge Him. Praise God.

We'd rented this camcorder (one that used a VHS tape)
to record this whole thing, so we go down to the milk barn
with my oldest half-sister taking us on a tour of the farm.
She said, "Well, let's go and see if they're down here." Sure
enough, my mom (Mama Liz) is in between her two brothers; her big brother Larry and her little brother Faye. Larry
and Faye, they're both married to the farm; they've been
married to the farm their whole life.

When I think of my dad that raised me and the snapshot
of him that's printed on my heart; it's my dad with his Bible
in his lap and his pipe in his mouth. Lori's dad, too, he's
in the Word (the Bible). It's the first thing he does in the
morning and the last thing he does before he goes to sleep.
When I got to see Lori's dad the first time, I thought this
is all too uncanny how God puts things together. You can
put the family that raised me, the family that gave me life,
and the family that is my life right now in one big salad
bowl, and it's all good! Lori's dad is my hero spiritually.
He inspired me to want to get back in the Word. He doesn't
know how many times he's read the Bible. God, I want to
be like that! I was listening to "Focus on the Family" (a

Christian radio program) one morning. They said, "When God's hand moves on the hearts of people. It's because other people prayed." I shared this one night with Lori's dad, and he slapped me on the shoulder and said, "What do you think?! I might not be the only one, but I'm one." I know I'm home because a lot of people prayed, and I know he's one. This is before meeting my mom. I'm reading along through my Bible, and I get in Psalm 139. I dare you to read Psalm 139:13-16 and not be amazed! It's like Jesus speaking directly to you saying, "(Your name here) guess what, I love you," that's the way this comes out. When I read this, I knew where I came from, and I knew how I was molded and shaped.

My mom had written this letter to the Lund Home. My mom and dad that raised me, saw the letter. It said something like, "I know that I'm not supposed to be able to have the favor asking for anything, but if it is your desire, would you please see that my son gets raised in a good Christian country home, where there are values of faith and love?" I thought it was so cool to tell my mom, "You got your wish." To be able to say that and mean it was so powerful.

It was our twenty-year reunion at the Military school. There were six of us standing in this little circle. We were a pretty tight group when we were in school. We were talking, and I said, "Wouldn't it be cool if Colonel Edmundson walked in here? What if he just walked up, like he always did, grabbed me by the back of the neck in that loving way he always did." Right when I said that, one guy elbows me, and he said, "Look, right there," and it was Colonel Edmundson. He talked to each of us. When I got to have my second with him, I said, "Colonel, you can deny it if you want; you could tell me I'm lying, or you don't even have to acknowledge it, but everything in me knows for all that we ever saw of you, and how good you made us feel, something in me knows we don't have any idea the hours you spent kneeling somewhere, bawling your eyes out over us, just so that we turned out halfway good. I want you to know that it worked." He hugged me and simply said, "I know."

Scripturally, who I am is written in 1 Corinthians 15:57, "Thanks be to God! He gives us victory through our Lord Jesus Christ." I live a victorious life; that's who I am. Why I live; what I am here for is written in Luke 22:32, "But I have prayed for you (your name here) that your faith may not fail. And when you have turned back, strengthen your brothers (and sisters)." Everybody appears in the Bible; you are in the Bible. I don't care who you are or what your station in life might be. You are in the Bible. Your mission is in there; your calling is in the Bible. So, you've got to pay attention.

If I had to give a twenty-second testimony, it would be to say, "I'm the product of God's grace; a mother's love; my parents' desire; a heart filled with grace, faith, and love; and a bride that loves me despite the goofy things I do."

Linda

I spoke with Linda over the phone, and she was happy to tell me about her cousin, JJ. She fondly remembers his reunion with his birth mom (Mama Liz). Although they are years apart in age and separated by distance, JJ and Linda seem remarkably close friends. I appreciate Linda sharing her perspective with us here.

Linda's Story, JJ's Cousin Through His Adoptive Family

JJ's mother, who raised him, was my father's sister. We've always stayed connected, JJ and me.

He is much younger than I am. I remember the house in Peru, New York, where they lived. My uncle Malcolm, his father, built apple storage buildings. He was smart about a lot of things. I went up there one summer to help a little bit when JJ (John) was a baby. I remember them trying to potty-train him. His older sister, who was adopted, was a little more of a challenge for my aunt. And I was too young to really intervene. I remember from the moment I met JJ as a baby, he always had a smile on his face. He just was born with a happy personality. And then they moved to New Mexico. So, he grew up there. I was out there one time; I think he was going to military school by then. But I do remember going around in the backfield on their place in Albuquerque. JJ was extremely attached to my immediate family. We grew up on a farm in upstate New York, and my mom and dad were great people. Everybody always liked to come back to the farm. My brother was five years younger than me, and I know JJ idolized him back then. When they would visit, we would play at the pond. And he was probably fishing because Uncle Malcolm loved to go fishing. We have lots of special memories growing up.

The fun thing for me was JJ meeting his birth mother. Jack, my husband, was alive at the time, and we had property in Vermont. JJ told us it was going to happen, and I knew where she worked, so I said, "Well, this restaurant would be an easy spot for you to meet because she'll know where it is." My husband thought it was funny, asking me, "Why do you want to go?" I said, "Because I'm the only one that JJ knows." It was a beautifully tender moment. We got there before JJ and Lori because they were flying in. It was right around Mother's Day. They weren't there yet, but when Jack and I drove in, I could see this couple in the car talking. I'm looking at her face, and I knew it was her. You could not help seeing her relationship with JJ! I chatted with them for a few minutes. I told her, "He'll probably come in wearing a ten-gallon hat and his cowboy boots." Which he did. They came pulling in, and JJ met his biological mom, and it went well. We all had a good conversation. He's still so easygoing. And his mom and her husband are really nice people. Jack and I thought they might stay with us that night, but they all went to her place. I think his mom and her husband have two daughters, and eventually, they did get to connect.

When JJ and Lori were here a couple of years ago for my brother's memorial service, we met his biological mother and husband again, and they stayed a couple of days together before heading home. Regarding JJ's biological father, I asked him once what happened. I think he knows his name and that he's a pretty healthy person, but JJ hasn't searched for him. The father who raised him will always be JJ's hero. He was a good daddy who loved him and wanted the best for him along the way.

He has a close relationship with his mom. I'm so happy for them.

1. JJ and his mom who raised him
2. JJ's dad who raised him
3. JJ and Mama Liz meeting for the first time
4. Mama Liz, JJ, Lori and Papa Wayne

Doris

This is my first daughter's story of her adoption. Our reunion happened only a year ago (2020). I am thrilled to include her words along with my own and those of my husband, Don, here.

Doris's Story

My adoption story might be a little different from other people, but probably pretty similar as well. I was adopted by my mom when I was two months and four days old. Before my adoption, I was in foster care, and judging from what I've been told about the state I was in when I was adopted, they didn't take the best care of me. According to my mom, I was a little dirty, exhausted (apparently, I slept for sixteen hours once I got home), and I pushed her away when she tried to give me affection. My adoptive mother took very good care of me. She was able to get me on a sleep schedule, kept me impeccably clean, dressed me in the frilliest clothes you ever saw, and patiently got me to where I no longer completely rebuffed affection.

As I grew up, I was a pretty happy kid, and I always knew I was adopted. I never had one of those *"omg"* moments like you see on TV where someone finds out they were adopted, and their world is turned upside down. My mom and grandmother embraced the fact that I was adopted and talked to me about it from a very early age, probably before I had any clue what they were talking about. My adoption day was always a big deal, too. We called it my Special Day, and it was like another birthday. I would get presents, and my mom would tell me the story of my adoption. I screamed all the way from Saint Louis to Cape Girardeau, slept for sixteen hours once they got me home, didn't want to take naps, wasn't on a schedule.

Growing up, I always knew I was different, and it didn't bother me too much. All my friends knew I was adopted, and they were just as chill about it as I was. It just was what it was. Part of me was always envious of my friends, though. Especially the ones who looked like their mom, dad, or siblings. I was the only one who looked like me. I have an older sister, but she was also adopted from a different family. The thought of having someone who looked like you and knowing exactly where you come from was always something I desperately wanted. Something that is an after-thought to most people seemed so incredibly important and just as much out of reach for me.

While it was relatively normal and happy, my childhood was not without its tribulations. My mom and my adoptive father were married when I was adopted but divorced when I was three years old. As a result, I don't remember a time when we lived together as a family. When I was three, we moved from Festus, Missouri, to Cape Girardeau, Missouri, where my grandparents lived. The situation surrounding their divorce was very messy and also involved some pretty severe mental health problems on the part of my adoptive father. He was actually an inpatient in a psych ward when my mom packed up our stuff, and we left for Cape.

The relationship with my adoptive father afterward was very inconsistent and unstable for the remainder of my childhood. He would come to pick us up for a day or a weekend every once in a while. I remember some of those visits being a lot of fun, usually when he was married, and his wife helped take care of us and made sure we felt welcomed and had fun. I also remember times when it wasn't as much fun. My dad's mental health was not great, like I mentioned, and I think sometimes it was worse than others. By the time I was about thirteen years old, I remember writing my dad a letter explaining how I felt and how the inconsistent relationship we had affected me. Pretty much from that point forward, I had very sporadic contact with him. I remember the last time I saw him. I was twenty-one and recently engaged to my now husband of fourteen years, whom I took with me for emotional support.

Unfortunately, that relationship never did repair itself, and it probably won't, but that's okay. Although I was definitely lacking a male figure to take care of me while I was growing up, I found that unconditional love and support in my husband, we married in 2007. My adopted mom has also been a constant source of love and support for me throughout my life. Despite this, however, I have always felt something was lacking in my life. It's hard to describe, but I just always felt like a piece of me was missing. I never felt completely understood by my adopted family. I have always felt a little different and more open-minded than the family I grew up in.

I have often thought of my birth parents over the years. I wondered what they looked like, who they were as people, did they care about me, did they think about me? All normal questions for an adopted person, I'm sure. I remember in high school, I volunteered at Birthright for a while, thinking how powerful it was that I could have been an unwanted baby that could have been aborted. That was one of the first times I remember just being *grateful* for the difficult decision that my birth mother made to give birth and then give me away. I knew back then that this could not have been an easy decision, and I was happy that she had chosen life for me.

As an adult, I have wondered time and time again about my birth parents, and I grappled with the decision of whether or not to try and find them. I kept telling myself it wasn't the right time because I didn't really know where to start, and I also felt like this would be a betrayal to my adopted mother. I felt that for me to wonder about my birth parents and to connect with them would somehow undermine all the love and care that my mom has given me throughout my life. I put my own needs on the back burner because I didn't want to hurt her.

A few years ago, after a lot of talks about this with my husband, he started digging a little bit, and he came across something that closed adoption records were going to be opened in the state of Missouri for a limited amount of time. He made sure I was okay with it, and he requested my original birth certificate. He received it a few months later, but he didn't say anything to me. He knew that I would ask about it when I was ready. Needless to say, the piece of paper that held the missing puzzle piece of my life just sat in his desk drawer for about a year before I told him I wanted to know more.

Several months later and my husband talked me into doing one of those genetic testing kits, which I did because I thought it might be cool to find out more about my ancestry and genetics. This is something that people from natural families take for granted—just knowing their family history. I knew little, except the few lines on each of my parents that was provided by the adoption agency. We did the genetic testing around Thanksgiving 2019 and got the results back close to Christmas. Much to my surprise, I had a match for my father. That was unexpected! So now I had a name, but not much else. Again, I dragged my feet to move forward with anything. I found out later that my husband had clicked the "connect" button, which sent a message to my birth father that I wanted to connect.

When I found out my birth father's name, it re-ignited the fire in me a little, and I then wanted to know my birth mom's name too. My husband showed me all the documents he had been saving for me once I was ready. My birth mother's full name and my original name were both on there. I was named "Angela Marie." I cried when I saw that my birth mom's middle name was also "Marie." I don't know why, but that small gesture meant so much to me. It showed me that she loved me. I also thought it was so uncanny that my given name was Angela because my middle name is Ann, and, as a grade-schooler, I went through a phase where I wanted everyone to call me "Annie."

I looked her up on Facebook and was surprised at how much I look like her. It was an amazing thing to *look* like someone else because this was always something I had wished for. I told myself I was going to reach out to her via Facebook messenger, but in true form, I procrastinated. I was afraid of rejection. I saw that she had two other children, and I realized that it might not be a good thing to have me re-enter the picture. Plus, it was the week of Christmas, and I didn't want to "ruin" her holidays. Looking back on this now, it seems silly, and I wish I would have just reached out.

So, nothing much happened with any of this until March 11, 2020, when my birth father finally checked his email and saw the notification I (my husband) had sent. He reached out to me, and we began talking. He also asked me if it was okay for him to tell my birth mom that he had found me, and I said yes. So, he and I kept talking and trying to get to know each other, and my birth mom reached out to me about two days later.

I will just say that my relationship with my birth father is complicated and is still a work in progress for sure. But my relationship with my birth mom has absolutely flourished. I was able to meet her in person a few weeks after we started texting. I was nervous and unsure how she felt about me at first. I guess I was also unsure of how I felt about her. Our husbands did a lot of the talking that first meeting, but I did take away a few things that showed me this could really be something real. The first was that she had told me that she felt like her mother, who passed away a few years ago, had a hand up in heaven of bringing us together. That felt powerful and meaningful to me. The next was that, before she left, she wanted to go say goodbye to my two little boys. My boys were nine and four at that time and, of course, are my whole world. It meant a lot to me that she wanted to start building that relationship with them too.

Over the last year, we have gotten together regularly to swim, play games, go for walks, build gingerbread houses, go to the pumpkin patch, have dinner, spend holidays together, watch the boys play ball—normal "family" stuff. She and her husband have integrated into our family in a way that I wouldn't have thought possible. It has been a wonderful experience for me, my boys, and my husband. I truly feel like we have gained a "bonus family" and are blessed to have them in our lives. I feel loved and accepted by them, and that part of my heart that has been missing my whole life is in the process of healing.

Rosanne's Story, Birth Mom

Here's one part of my story; it formed who I am. Looking back now, I see God was in the midst of it even when I thought He wasn't there.

I was only sixteen when I found out I was pregnant. I thought I was in love. That's an age when you think you know everything. I couldn't have been more wrong. I remember how hurt and (frankly) embarrassed my mom was when I told her. And that was a horrible feeling, disappointing her.

During my pregnancy, I felt deep shame whenever someone gave me *that* look; maybe you've experienced it too. Is it pity or judgment? Maybe you've looked at someone that way. I'm sure I have without even realizing it. There are places where one hopes the people will show compassion; for me, it was our church and my Christian high school. Instead, I was met with judgment, and it felt as though I was surrounded by hypocrites. I stopped attending church, which I am sure further broke my mom's heart. Her faith was everything to her. I felt as if God was rejecting me, too, just as many people in my life had. So many emotions; shame, embarrassment, fear, and the reality that no one could understand or seemed willing to try.

During my pregnancy, my boyfriend and I saw each other occasionally. Only ever at home, we never went out in public together. His parents were always kind to me. We broke up after our daughter was born and have since spoken only once, about eight years ago, simply because we were each curious if the other had heard anything about Angela. We exchanged phone numbers "just in case" either of us did. And in my mind, I felt that time would probably never arrive. Ours was a closed adoption, which means the birth parents cannot get any information unless the child seeks them out through the organization that arranged the adoption.

On May 26, 1985, one month to the day after I turned seventeen, I gave birth to a baby girl. I named her Angela Marie. At that moment, everything melted away except the pure joy of holding her. I believed it would be the first and last time I would see her in my lifetime.

I decided that Angela would be adopted. It was, undoubtedly, the most difficult thing I'd ever done and probably still is to this day. Taking the "easy" way out and having an abortion was never an option, for my Catholic upbringing was so ingrained in me. I had to trust God's plans for her and for me. Thankfully, after the initial shock, my mom was super supportive. Although, I'll never fully know the emotional impact this experience had on her. We rarely talked about it afterward. I guess we both grieved the loss and kept looking forward.

Living in that loss (and more), I went looking to fill a hole in my heart. Of course, now I know, no person can do that; only God can, but not back then. I wanted to feel loved and went in search of it in the wrong places.

I finished high school at the same Christian school. The entire situation, my daughter, was never brought up again. I went on to college, and that's where I met the man who would be my husband. I let him know pretty much right away about Angela, figuring if he wasn't okay with who I was, then at least I'd know before it got serious. Fortunately, God has a plan for us, and Don and I are still together thirty-two years later.

I am happy in my life. Don and I have two adult children and built a wonderful life together. Yet my shame remained buried. I could never forget there's a piece of my-self out there, and I had no idea where. So many questions I thought would not be answered. I thought of her so often through the years. What was she like? Was she happy? So, I prayed for her, asking God, again and again, to watch over her because I could not. This prayer brought me some com-fort. Somewhere inside, a small nugget of my faith could not be completely extinguished.

Still, I didn't go back to church for over twenty years.

God found an unexpected route to bring me back to Him. By surrounding me with people of strong faith, God stirred my desire for more of Him. About this same time, two friends invited me to attend their church, and I went. The first time I stepped through those doors, I felt like I was home. I became a member of that church, served in the children's ministry, and in 2013 I reaffirmed my faith. For the first time, I chose for myself.

We all suffer losses; it's part of our human experience. In 2017, my mom went to heaven, and then in 2019, my (step) dad joined her there. In the past few years, I've al-lowed myself to stay stuck in my grief, still not fully able to process everything. Mom visited me in a *dream* not long after she went to heaven, and her words have stuck with me ever since, "Do your very best." Every time I think I've figured out what she meant, something else shows up, and I think maybe that's the thing to which she referred. Turns out there's not one thing. She knows *all* the challenges ahead of me. So, for better or worse, I will do my absolute best caring for my family, dealing with illness and grief, building relationships, *living life*! That's what Mom meant for me all along; it's the way she lived her life as an example for us.

Little did I know, God continued to arrange things for me.

Quite unexpectedly, on March 11, 2020, as I'm preparing to leave the house for a funeral visitation, I received a message from Angela's birth father. He and she were matched on a DNA test site. What he sent me was a screenshot of the message he received, which said "daughter." Her name and photo were also visible. To say I was in shock would be true. Incredulous. I almost couldn't believe what I was seeing. I am so grateful he chose to share this revelation with me.

Astonishingly, after thirty-four years, I knew what Angela's name was now, Doris; with a few keystrokes, I could see her face! And she looks so much like me; it was surreal. I just don't know how else to express it. I immediately shared the news with my sister and my husband. Both of them were extremely excited and wanting to know when I would reach out to her. First, I needed a bit of time (it only took me forty-eight hours) to just sit with this news. One of my first thoughts of the hundreds that were racing through my mind at light speed was my mom and how much I wished she were here to meet our girl again. Then just as quickly, I knew Mom had somehow helped make this hap-

pen; after all, she'd been watching over me and knew Doris
and her family from heaven for three years now. Thanks,
Mom. I really needed something positive and joy-filled in
my life. God's timing is always perfect.

Before I could move forward and meet Doris and her
family, I needed to tell Don and my children they have a
sister. I had tucked that part of my life away for so long and
didn't know quite how or when to bring it up with them
as they were growing up. The last thing I ever wanted to
do was hurt my children's feelings. This is no small thing,
learning you have a sister. They are both adults now, so I
needed to trust in their love and acceptance and God's timing. Our son is an open book; knowing this, I talked with
him first. He was curious and asked some questions and
said he'd like to meet Doris sometime. On the other hand,
our daughter keeps her feelings close and can be difficult
to read. I was afraid she might feel threatened like Doris
would take her place; I honestly had no idea how she might
react. I plucked up my courage and talked with our daughter, and I was pleasantly surprised by her reaction. She
asked some questions and told me she was happy for me.
Whew! I felt such a sense of relief.

I now know Doris is okay and happy in her life. It's
all I ever wanted for her. My joy in growing a relationship
with Doris and her family is beyond expression. After a few
weeks of messages, we found a time to meet in person. Yes,
I was extremely nervous. I feel like she was, too, because
our husbands did a lot of the talking at first. They are both
encouraging us to develop our relationship. This was also

when I met my two grandsons, then ages nine and four, for the first time. These boys fill my heart to overflowing when I'm with them! Oh, how I've longed to be a grandma! In those first few months, we regularly visited for dinners and swimming in their pool. We attended the boys' baseball and T-ball games and got to meet Doris' mom at one of the games (unfortunately, only from a distance because it was the beginning of COVID-19). In 2020, we celebrated our first Christmas together, and I look forward to so many more to come.

I am no longer ashamed. In bringing Doris back into my life, God orchestrated the perfect way to erase my shame. He gave me my voice back! Each time I share my story with someone new, I realize again how free I feel though I never recognized that my shame had imprisoned me. It is miraculous, and I want to shout it from the rooftops. Now, I realize what I did took immense courage, and I am proud to share my story. Now, I feel love, acceptance, and freedom. My hope is that, by telling my story, it will be a blessing to others no matter which side of the adoption story they are on.

Doris looks like me and, amazingly, we like many of the same activities. I eagerly anticipate many heart-to-heart talks. I chose from the beginning that I'd allow her to lead in our relationship. I'm following along, however fast or slow. There is no book to read illustrating how to navigate this unique relationship; these are uncharted waters. It is one day at a time. Our bond will flourish in its own time. (It seems to grow stronger each time we are together.) There is a myriad of emotions showing up for both of us to work through, and I'm confident we will navigate these. I will be forever grateful for this unexpectedly wonderful opportunity to know my first daughter and become a part of her family again. This chapter of my story has been written all along; I just had to catch up to it.

This year (2021), around Mother's Day, I wrote and mailed a heartfelt letter to Doris' mom. I wished only to express the depth of my gratitude to her for doing what I was not able to do; be a mom for this child, our precious daughter. And to let her know how much I want to be part of her family. I truly hope that one day God will open her heart to the possibility of knowing me because I want desperately to know her and hear all the stories of Doris growing up.

Today, although it's been just over one year since we met again, it feels like Doris and her family have always been part of our family. Thankfully, they only live an hour's drive from our home. We visit often and are creating new memories with Doris, her husband, and their two boys. It's better than I could have ever imagined!

Not long ago, the five-year-old described our connection (adoption) to me this way, "You had Mom and gave her to Grandma." Yep! That's how it happened. Kids have a way of making things so simple, don't they?

Don

We met in 1986 in college. We were "just friends" that year because I was dating someone else. (That boyfriend broke up with me once summer came.) When the school year ended in May, and as everyone was packing up to head home, I went looking for Don at the dorm to say goodbye, but he was already gone. I found out that the dorm would forward mail to his home address but wouldn't give that address to me directly. I went home and wrote Don a letter. I know he still has it (and all the others from that summer), and I've no idea what I said. (Yes, I have all the ones he wrote back.) Don and I became "pen pals" and kept our friendship alive. That fall, he returned to college, and I did not. Luckily, I went to visit some friends, and we ran into each other again. We started dating in 1987 and have been together ever since. Why did I write that first letter? Now, I can't even recall. Somehow, deep down, I recognized that I needed him in my life. And the rest, as they say, is history. He is my true love, my best friend, and my fellow adventurer in this life. I am grateful for his willingness to tell our story from his unique perspective; the husband of someone reunited with a child that came before. His acceptance and love are greater than I could ever imagine.

Don's Story, Rosanne's Husband

I've always known that my wife had a daughter. Out there in the world somewhere. She told me early on in our relationship. I don't remember exactly how she said it, but at the time, it sounded to me a bit like a challenge, as in how was I going to respond to that. Or maybe it was just fair warning. I had no problem with that; in fact, I don't remember that it even gave me pause. We had already been friends for about a year, and we were not so much dating as easing into a relationship that already felt very natural to me.

When you're young, of course, the passage of time seems much greater than it does today. It had been just a little over two years since she gave birth. Back then, that seemed a world away to me, so I didn't think about it deeply. Looking back now, I realize how raw that must have still felt for her.

We married about a year and a half later, and we had our son at a young age. Thus, we dove into life, and again, her earlier pregnancy seemed a world away.

Over the years, we would discuss her daughter maybe once a year. Almost always, when we were on a long drive somewhere, either on a road trip vacation or heading home to Missouri from the far corner of Georgia (where we were stationed with the military). (We've always had our best conversations on long car trips.) It was almost always me who brought up this particular subject. It just seemed important, this unexplored and unresolved part of her. We would talk about it for a bit, as much as she cared to talk, and then let it go for another year. It's only now that I realize how much more her daughter was actually on her mind. I remember that Rosanne thought of her as Angela, and I knew who the bio-dad was (which was always accompanied by a twinge of jealously), but not much else. I never thought to ask what day Angela's birthday was, though now

I believe that day was on Rosanne's mind every year. And that she thought of Angela much more often, probably almost daily. But she never shared that, though I would have been happy to have her open up.

The one exception was about ten years ago when Rosanne decided to contact the adoption agency and let them know that she'd be open to connecting with her daughter. That was a glimmer of hope, but nothing came of it, and the subject faded into the background again.

Up to that point, I had always figured that someday, somehow, we would learn who the daughter was and possibly reconnect. But after that, though I wasn't conscious of it, I started to feel more that it wasn't ever going to happen. Almost as if we'd lost someone from our lives, even though we didn't know who that person was. I pondered a few times what I would do if (far in the future) Rosanne passed before me, and I was left with a choice of whether to tell our kids that they had an older sister somewhere because Rosanne had never shared that with them.

It would be fair to ask why this was important to me. I love my wife totally, and my main feeling about her having given up a child for adoption is that I would love to know this person, who is very much a part of Rosanne, a missing piece. And I hoped for Rosanne to have some closure.

The moment when Rosanne told me that she'd found her daughter was one of those surreal moments when you learn something so monumental that it takes a minute for your mind to even comprehend the words. When your first response is simply "What?" because the news didn't fully process the first time. Emotionally, it was as big a moment for me as learning about being pregnant with each of our two kids, though different, of course. Even though Rosanne hadn't shared a lot, I had always imagined years of unanswered questions. And now, suddenly, there were answers. At least the first few, the tip of the iceberg.

Since then, I have been happy to discover how quickly and easily Doris (Angela) and her crew have come to feel like family. Almost immediately, as though they'd somehow been here the whole time. It would have been good for Rosanne to learn about her daughter regardless, but one point I'd never really given much thought to was that the daughter might have created a family of her own. In my mind, "Angela" was always a teenager or a young woman, not yet someone with kids of her own.

I'm not a people person. In meeting long-lost family, you don't know who they're going to be. So, it's such a relief to find that these are people I really like, beyond just the connection to Rosanne. The grandkids are a blast, just the best little kids you could imagine. My only disappointment is that we didn't connect sooner. Recently, I've had a sense, just a bit, that we've already missed much of the window for the older boy, who isn't really little anymore. The last time I saw him, I realized that he already seems more like a young man, just in the year we've known him. Time passes so quickly when you're talking about kids growing up, and it only takes a few years for them to lose interest in the family as they start to form their own lives.

The last year has been one of the richest of our lives, despite what else might be going on in the world. More than anything, because of this reconnection. The timing was what it needed to be for Rosanne. When we were younger, I loved how joyful she often was. That hasn't seemed so true in recent years for several reasons. Reconnecting with her daughter has come at a time when it was sorely needed, I think, and I am grateful for that.

My own family life has always been a divided one, though not specifically in the same way as Doris'. While I don't know how she feels about that personally, I do have a strong sense of some of the ways that she might feel. I've wanted to caution Rosanne (and sometimes I have) not to do too much too fast because of feeling like the whole connection might just break like so much glass. Thankfully, I've been wrong about that. And even though Doris has her adopted family with a lot more history, it is especially important to me that, as time goes by, she comes to feel like we are also fully her family, that we're fully here for her and Simon and their kids.

I'm immensely proud of my wife, not for specific things she's done (though the inspiration and creation of this book are pretty cool!), but for more fundamentally who she is as a person, someone I'm grateful to be able to spend my life with. She's incredibly determined and one of the most fundamentally good and loving people you could ever meet. So, on the one hand, I don't think there was ever any question of whether or not she would have the unexpected child. But on the other hand, I know she struggled with the decision to give her up for adoption. Had she not, of course, none of us would be where we are, or would even be at all. It has been my privilege to have a front-row seat in this real-life story of being reunited.

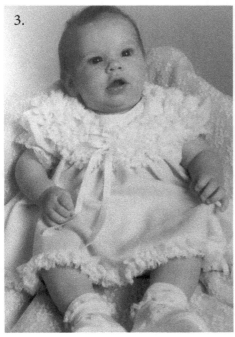

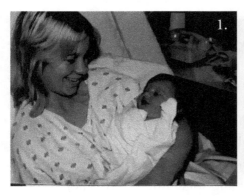

1. Rosanne holding Angela (Doris) when she was born
2. My three babies and me; Morgan, Brendan, Rosanne and Doris
3. Doris at 6 months old
4. Don with our grandsons

Afterword

Since reuniting with my first daughter, I have read many books and have many more on my list. I've sought out insights and advice from experts in those books, on multiple podcasts, and in person. I am learning about the unique challenges adoptees and their families face. I am also learning about the abundant love and heartbreak surrounding adoption.

I acknowledge those people who remain disconnected from their birth families, whether they are actively searching without success or have chosen not to search for their own reasons. And those who have been reunited and, unfortunately, it wasn't the happy reunion they had hoped it would be. May our stories offer you hope!

I can honestly say that after my first daughter was well past the age when she could've sought me out, and I'd heard nothing, my hope waned. Still, I prayed that one day the timing would be right, and I would get to meet her.

My prayer for you, if you are in that place of not knowing, is that you will have peace in the waiting because one day, whether here on Earth or in heaven, you will be reunited!

"When I thought I lost me / You knew where to find me / You reintroduced me to Your Love / You picked up all my pieces / Put me back together / You are the defender of my heart" (Francesca Battistelli, "Defender").

A Short List of Resources

The books listed here are ones I've personally read to understand more about my own experience and that of my first daughter. There are, of course, numerous books and resources available on this subject.

Berry, Mike and Kristin. *Securely Attached: How Understanding Childhood Trauma Will Transform your Parenting.* (Also, look for *The Honestly Adoption* podcast.)

Newton Verrier, Nancy. *The Primal Wound: Understanding the Adopted Child.*

Eldridge, Sherrie. *Twenty Things Adopted Children Wish their Adoptive Parents Knew.*

To learn more about the *Ghost Kingdom*: books by Betty Jean Lifton, including:

Lifton, Betty Jean. *Lost and Found: The Adoption Experience.*

Several contributors connected through various websites, including:

www.23 andme.com

www.adoption.com

www.ancestry.com

For those considering adoption, visit my friend Marcy Bursac's site:

www.forgottenadoptionoption.com

Read her book: *The Forgotten Adoption Option: A Self-reflection and How-to Guide for Pursuing Foster Care Adoption.* (Find her podcast on her website.)